Contents

Flinging before it sizzling bolts of lightning, a summer thunderstorm marches across Tonto Basin en route to the Mogollon. FRANK ZULLO

Introduction

A s a young boy I was brought to Arizona by a father seeking relief from cruelly painful arthritis. Our move came only a short spell after the American Southwest's own adolescence. A baker's dozen of us Boy Scouts — chaperoned by a schoolteacher at the wheel of a borrowed, battered school bus — had made camp at Grand Canyon, and now we were drifting homeward. Half my companions were impoverished Pima Indians whose forebears, as volunteer militia, scouted and routed enemy renegade red men.

Back then, there were Boston suburbs containing more citizens than all of Arizona. In 1940 the federal census enumerated 499,261 residents. If Arizonans were sprinkled over the map evenly like shaken pepper, only four people would occupy a square mile. About half of Arizona's people in those days huddled together in three or four towns, and counties bigger than Connecticut counted populations the size of a large high school.

On our return trip, we very nearly reduced Arizona's population by 14.

Our bus was one of those 1930-something lemon yellow pumpkins with a high center of gravity and oily brakes. Of course

The Mogollon Rim Country

A WORLD APART

there were no seat belts. Our gear, including geology samples, canned goods, and iron cookware was stowed in the overhead book racks. About 10 miles southwest of Long Valley, the unpaved washboard logging road reached the abrupt edge of the regional Colorado Plateau. Conifer-clad, the Mogollon Rim at that point rises some 8,000 feet above sea level, and the angle of repose approximates 90 degrees — meaning that toward the center of the planet, the force of mass for ages had relentlessly tugged. So

(RIGHT) An Aphrodite butterfly pauses to perch upon a Rim Country wildflower.
FRANK ZULLO
(LEFT) A morning campfire perfumes the clear air of a Rim's edge campsite.
NICK BEREZENKO
(FOLLOWING PANEL) Crimson box elders burst into autumn dress, while quaking aspens have nearly spent all of their golden dollars.
LARRY ULRICH

everything loose (including buses) tended to slip and congregate as detritus upon the shaky alluvial fans which buttressed vertical cliffs.

In the 1880s when Revilo (Oliver spelled backward) Fuller freighted this hill, he would fell a virgin ponderosa pine, chain the bole to his rear axle, and drag it down the 1,000-foot drop to Strawberry village. This kept his wagon from overrunning his team. On the extremely steep grades he would slip logs through the spokes to lock the wheels. In the 1940s this road was not much improved since it was surveyed by Fuller's mules.

Well, we pitched off The Rim piloted by our teacher accustomed to driving the level desert at Casa Grande. (Geographically speaking, Casa Grande could serve as proper headquarters for the International Flat Earth Society.) We hit the first turn about 20 mph too fast, as simultaneously we boys made a rush to the right side for an eagle's view of Strawberry Valley. The driver jumped the brakes hard, a shoe grabbed, tires slid, and a solid ton of boys pressed against the glass. The bus nearly swapped ends, while our Feather Merchant driver spun the wheel in the manner of playing bumper tag in a carnival ride. Somehow we didn't tip as the tires flipped gravel over the edge. And by some miracle our helmsman wrenched the vehicle into a right bend carved out of a sedimentary shelf. Unsheathed axes, tents, and all manner of camping gear cascaded from the overhead racks onto our heads. Thirteen lads thereupon fell as sodden dolls against the *left* window panes, to watch a hundred yards of limestone slide by, six inches from our noses. Our teacher never did gain full control of the bus until we arrived in the swale of Strawberry.

White as bone, the teacher trembled out of the door and went inside a small store that displayed an A-1 Beer sign. We kids stood around. After a long absence, our teacher eventually emerged with an armload of frosty Barqs strawberry drinks. I detected on his breath a certain yeasty aroma.

Twenty miles more down the road, with crimson tongues and a goofy professor, we eased into Payson, a false-front cowtown beside itself with the "August Doin's" — that was, rodeo, as it was in the beginning. Bulldoggin'. Steer ropin'. Horse races on Main Street. Pretty girls in tight Levi's. Genuine cowboys.

Such was my introduction to The Rim Country. And may this anecdote help to explain why, a half-century later, when people ask about my feelings for this country, I tell them I love The Rim the way a poor, scared, dry-mouthed Indian boy off the alkali desert loves an ice-cold Barqs soda pop on a summer day.

With the exception of Grand Canyon, Arizona's most impressive landform is the Mogollon Rim. It scribes the abrupt southern edge of the vast, four-state Colorado Plateau. Geologist Halka Chronic tells us:

"Here on the Colorado Plateau a great block of the earth's crust has remained coherent and recognizable through 600 million years and more, while blocks around it have been tilted and squeezed and broken.... There seems to be some sort of underlying difference here, a difference that has lasted through much of the earth's history, as if the more or less circular patch of the earth's crust that makes up the Plateau obeyed a different set of geologic rules."

Starting in far northwestern Arizona and angling to a point south of Flagstaff, sheer cliffs begin to show themselves in the Sycamore and Oak Creek Canyon area. The Rim then curves east by southeast more than 200 miles and extends well into New Mexico as the Mogollon Mountains. All along this sharp crustal edge Mother Earth parades a combination of typical features: relatively flat plateau cut by north-flowing streams...near vertical cliffs dropping hundreds of feet...then a jumble of steep-sloped talus and massif drained by a series of watercourses running generally south and west.

So formidable is this escarpment, it was given wide berth by intrepid Spanish soldiers and priests who otherwise busily poked around the region during the two centuries preceding the founding of the United States. Of this fastness, a 50-mile-wide heartland was not much populated until the 1960s, '70s, and '80s. Even today the largest community of the central Mogollon counts fewer than 9,000 citizens.

The Rim is named for Juan Ignacio Flores Mogollon, governor of New Mexico which, in the early 1700s under Spanish rule, included Arizona. According to Delia Sanchez, teacher of Spanish at Phoenix Community College, the proper articulation of Mogollon is Mo (as in mow the grass), go (the g hard as in the English "go", and the last syllable an accented YAWN (as when you're sleepy). Self-appointed Spanglish authority, folklorist James E. Cook, declares that the most common *norteamericano* rendition is "Muggy-OWN," as in, "It's *muggy* today, and I'm glad I *own* a cabin on The Rim."

This middle section of the Mogollon now and then goes by another, more easily pronounced nickname, The Tonto Rim, or simply, "The Rim." This highland occasionally is called Zane Grey Country.

The most popular Western novelist before Louis L'Amour, Grey frequently retreated to his Arizona cabin during the first decades of the 20th century. Virtually roadless woodlands lay all about. Grey would recline in an overstuffed chair on a porch that hung like a scaffold over the Tonto Basin. Needing scenic description, he could lower his paper and absorb vistas of cotton cloud, endless forest, and steel-blue mountains.

"Westward along the Rim vast capes jutted out, differing in shape and length, all ragged sharp, fringed, reaching darkly for the gold and purple glory of the sunset. Shafts and rays of light streamed from the rifts in the clouds, blazing upon the rock faces of the wall. Eastward the Rim zigzagged endlessly into pale cold purple. Southward a vast green hollow ran like a river to the sea, to empty, it seemed, into space. Beyond that rose dim spectral shapes of mountains, remote and detached. To the north the great wall shut out what might lie beyond...."

Today Zane Grey Country is made more accessible by modern highways, but it remains much as it was when it inspired such sagas as *To the Last Man* and *Under the Tonto Rim.* By foresight and good fortune, the priceless qualities of The Rim largely have been preserved as national forest.

Gone are the Indian hunters, the hard-riding dragoons, the Spanish seekers of mineral riches, the wagon trains of settlers, the pioneer ranchers, the lonely shepherds, and the first of America's ecologists, federal foresters.

This is still the refuge of elk, deer, bear, and lion. You yet may ride a mount all day through certain of The Rim's mountain passes and never cross a paved road. The adventurous hiker can tackle a 50-mile-long trail with sure knowledge he will not smell engine exhaust fumes anywhere along the way.

In The Rim Country, history buffs can retrace the expeditions of early-day beaver trappers, stand at the site of an Indian massacre, touch the walls of a long-ago homestead, or visit the graves of victims of a bloody range war. The Rim country is a land big enough to welcome birdwatchers, picnickers, painters, campers, gem seekers, fishermen, and a few tired souls who simply want to withdraw to a sylvan glade.

Recently, the sentiment was voiced by a gent who retired and moved to Arizona from Delaware, where the highest elevation is Jerimoth Hill 812 feet above the sea. At first sight this newcomer bought a house in Payson, spent more than a summer exploring the country within a 50-mile radius, and bragged in a letter home:

"Folks, I didn't just buy a cabin. I bought a whole country!" ∎

RICK O'DELL

Phoenix free-lance writer, Don Dedera, a former editor of *Arizona Highways* magazine, has been writing about Southwestern subjects for 40 years. His production includes a thousand non-fiction articles and 15 books, notably, *A Little War of Our Own*, about a violent range feud that blazed through The Rim Country a century ago. Many of his essays have been about The Rim and Payson, where he and his wife, Nancy, make their second home.

Chapter One

T he Mogollon Rim Country!

Where in the West does a place contain more reality and romance of the last century's American frontier?

Here survive remnant forts from the Indian wars, honest-to-gosh working cow ranches, trails blazed by army scouts and mountain men, and against all odds, humble log cabins made comfortable by industrious damsels in olden days. Here too dwell descendants of Arizona's first pioneers, great-grandchildren of wagon train immigrants. And caretakers of artifacts left by ancient cultures, the U.S. Cavalry, Apache braves, gold prospectors, six-gun sheriffs, saloon girls, schoolmarms, and officers' ladies.

Here thrive three national forests that contribute sweeps of bounteous woodland to form the Massachusetts-sized portion called The Rim. For fortunate moderns, The Rim takes in a piece of outdoors with room enough for wilderness backpacking, ritual flyfishing, nature filming, history exploring, back road four-wheeling, overland skiing, productive gem-seeking, roadside picnicking, hobby gardening, rock climbing, and just plain stumpsitting.

Bigger, this area is, than many countries of the world. And if The Rim Country really were a country, the piney town of Payson

would be its capital.

Located near the geographical center of Arizona, Payson today is reached by several easy ways. But the most popular is State Route 87, often referred to locally as "the Beeline." Route 87 is a logarithmic improvement over the rutted wagon path of the 1880s, and a hundred times better than the dusty, corduroy car road of the 1950s that could consume six hours of driving and two tires in the drive from Phoenix.

Payson, as an American settlement, goes back not much more than a century, but about 1,500 years ago the town-site was home for prehistoric people classified by archaeologists as the Mogollon Culture. Thus far, some 50 archaeological sites have been identified within 2,000 acres of Tonto National Forest surrounding Payson.

As an engaging reminder of the first Americans, at Payson's southern entrance today prospers one of Arizona's smaller Indian reser-

Payson
GATEWAY TO THE RIM COUNTRY

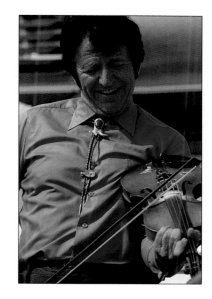

(LEFT) Never far removed from its primary transportation artery, State Route 87, Payson town casually sprawls out into its remnant groves of ponderosa, piñon, and oak.
MICHAEL COLLIER

(RIGHT) Played on fiddle or violin; mainly for dance, and with roots older than the 20th century--that's the kind of music heard at Payson's Old-time Fiddlers Contest.
JEFF KIDA

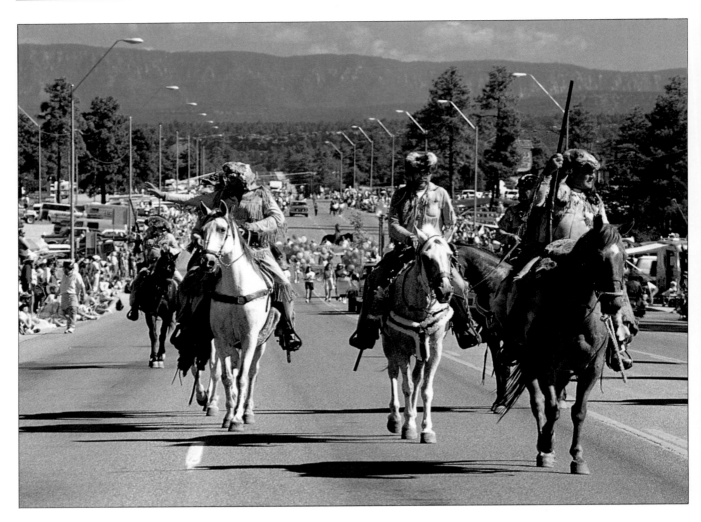

vations. The 100-member Tonto Apaches for nearly a century were dispossessed squatters, facing day-to-day eviction. Sympathetic, influential friends in 1972 persuaded Congress to set aside a desirable juniper-studded hillside. Today the tribe operates a construction firm, pursues craft arts, runs a store, and participates in Payson events.

The first whites to see Payson environs were soldiers on campaign and prospectors seeking gold and silver. By now, the wily, wiry Athabascan Apaches considered The Rim their motherland. Alertly guarding his scalp, William Burch, miner-rancher, operated the Golden Waif Mine in the area as early as 1878 and erected a stout cabin in 1883 on what is now Burch Mesa near today's Payson Airport. Burch's brand served as the only place name for a while. Nearby rises the remains of Fort McDonald, a stone-encircled hilltop fortified in 1878 as a community retreat during Indian uprisings. As settlement slowly increased, the place was known as Green Valley and Union Park, and since March 3,

1884, Payson, in honor of the Illinois senator who helped the village obtain a post office.

Impulse and derring-do continue as century-long Payson traditions. One legendary example: Following a double wedding, when the parties filed out of the office of the Payson justice of the peace one August day in 1890, Arizona Charley Meadows bellowed:

"It is my pleasure to offer, as my present to these newlyweds, that if all the parties in attendance will saddle up with their lariats and ride over my ranges, the brides and grooms can have any of my unbranded calves you can catch!"

(ABOVE) Bill Williams Mountain Men enliven Payson's annual rodeo parade.
(OPPOSITE PAGE, LEFT) A crosscut sawyer races through a pine bole, one of 21 events at the annual Loggers Sawdust Festival.
(TOP RIGHT) Apache Crown Dancers keep alive their ancient ceremonials. PHOTOS BY NICK BEREZENKO
(LOWER RIGHT) Arizona Charley Meadows. COURTESY SHARLOT HALL MUSEUM, JEAN KING COLLECTION

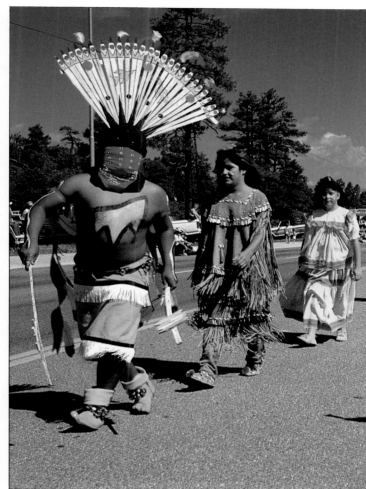

Rodeo! By the time the chaotic calf scramble concluded at dusk, 36 head of Charley's dogies had been roped and branded as starter stock for the two couples.

While Tombstone made news as Shoot-'em-up Junction, early Payson was more noted for good-natured drinking and dancing than street fighting. As Historian Marguerite Noble has written:

"Although Payson was not an unruly pioneer town, the saloons were highly patronized and often incited commotion. Rambunctious drunks were chained to a tree to sleep off their problems. The settlers were mainly peaceable families, colonizing and stabilizing new borders, but they were neither timid nor cowardly when the need came for them to take care of themselves.

"Jake Lane, a newcomer from Texas, left one of the saloons after an excessive drinking bout. He rode up and down the street, shooting his pistol. Myrle Evans and Myrth Jones, now 82...say they

were playing croquet with their friends when Jake ran his horse through their game 'scattering us like quail.' [One of the players was Judge William Colcord.] The judge advised Jake to put away his little shooter. Instead Lane pointed his gun at William Colcord. This was a mistake — and his last. Guns blasted. Lane toppled from his horse, dead from Colcord's Luger. The court cleared Colcord."

But for such an infrequent exception, a heritage of spontaneous generosity continues to permeate Payson's lifestyle. Hitchhikers wait not long. Payson drivers tend to wave at every other car. They blast their horns at friends. Western dress prevails: cowboy boots or hiking boots, everywhere denims. Maybe a Lexus some day will sell in the Payson area, but not until it's offered in a four-wheel-drive pickup truck configuration.

The ranching image is bona fide. Only in recent times was Payson encircled by the Town Fence to prevent range cattle from browsing the flower beds. But still at risk are vegetable gardens and orchards, routinely harvested by deer, javelina, and (look out!) a mama black bear with cubs. Unplanned in totally planned Payson West: On a recent morning the half-devoured remains of a coyote were found encircled by cougar tracks.

Payson's laid-back citizens make a living at a sizable sawmill and in cottage factories producing everything from whatnots to whirligigs. At times it seems half of Payson buys the other half of the town in interlocking swap meets, only to advertise the junk for sale the following weekend.

Subdivisions proliferate to shelter retirees and second-home owners (both working class and wealthy; Payson has an impressive number of million-dollar homes.) An accelerating number of Rim Country workers are flextimers, home-employed high techs who could live anywhere they can plug in their computer, modem, and fax. Some holidays the resident population of about 8,300 swells by maybe 20,000 flatland "furriners," counting those camping out nearby in the woods.

No doubt the air was intoxicating as wine before Payson was settled. It's as clean today as then, except for inverted wintry morns when wood stove smoke lingers in the pockets. In fact, *Sunbelt Retirement Magazine* identified Payson as one of the three healthiest places in the world to live: thanks to having one of only three Pure Ozone Belts in the world. Payson's mild, four-season climate typifies Arizona at about a mile high: temperatures averaging 15 to 20 degrees cooler than the deserts; an average 21 inches of annual precipitation, most falling between November and March. Three or four substantial snowfalls below The Rim usually melt swiftly, although at higher elevations a snowpack can last for weeks and months.

Celestial fireworks dominate the skies through July and August and into September as masses of moist air push northward from Mexico and ram into The Rim. During the summer rainy season at any time, but usually between midday and 3:00 p.m., cumulonimbus clouds boil to 40,000 feet and both entertain and astound with one of earth's superlative lightning displays. Psychedelic flashes, rolling bombinations, and drenching downpours scrub the skies. More than 200,000 lightning bolts were recorded of a recent Arizona August...the greater number striking along The Rim.

Where to begin enjoying Payson?

The town boasts that all other chambers of commerce pale in comparison to Payson's friendly ways. The tiny CofC anchors the north side of Main Street at the first traffic signal in the south section of town. Maps, brochures, advice, plain and fancy brags, gossip, and corn relish recipes available. Right in town:

Main Street — If parts seem like movie sets ...they've been used as such. Spirited horses of the Houston brothers used to sprint from the schoolhouse to the sawmill for as much as $1,200 on a side. Kaibab Industries runs the sawmill as Payson's biggest employer. The oldest building in Payson huddles as a watch fob adobe back of the Olla Lazear home. It was built for a Mr. Siddles by a Mr. Vogel for $30 in 30 days. Other structures along Main recently have been catalogued in an effort to qualify the street for the National Register of Historic Places.

The Museum of the Forest — Look for the sign reading "Home of Northern Gila County Historical Society Payson Museum." Dedicated in the autumn of 1990, the Museum of the Forest takes in two buildings of high importance to the area: the original Forest Service Ranger Station and the ranger residence. Obtained together with the site by an act of Congress, the museum is owned and administered by the NGCHS. The two older buildings have been lovingly restored. A unifying structure reminiscent of Payson's burned down Herron Hotel stands between the old frame edifices. The new museum houses public exhibits ranging from Zane Grey's saddle to historic quilts, from techniques of forest management to a working model of an old sawmill. Displays are changed often, so one visit is never enough.

Unique perhaps, and nifty as a perfect antique can be, stands the top 25 feet of the Forest Service lookout tower salvaged from the apex of Mount Ord south of Payson. It had been assembled in the 1930s by the soil soldiers of the Civilian Conservation Corps. The fire tower is outfitted with fire-sighting instruments, period telephone and other apparatus used by lookouts to spot and report hundreds of wildfires through more than five decades.

Payson's festivals — Expressed in its motto, "the town with the festivals," Payson fills the calendar with weekend events. Most notable, the "August Doin's," which since 1882 has been Payson's name for its oldest continuously held American rodeo. Here, insist Payson loyalists, rodeo began, and the range tournament enjoys official sanction by the Professional Rodeo Cowboys Association. On other dates there's an Old-timers Rodeo, a Loggers/Sawdust Fest celebrating The Rim Country's lumbering, pulpwood and forest products industries. Into its second decade the Payson Old Time Country Music Festival attracts pickers and grinners from everywhere. On other occasions Payson hosts a junior rodeo, a chili cook-off, arts shows, a square dance extravaganza, and a

Christmas lighting ceremony centered around the alpine-like Swiss Village.

So Payson's future seems as promising as its past was productive. If the folks can retain their spirit of community, it will always be a place for visitors to kick back and relax, or get up and go, as in the days when Zane Grey himself played and worked, under the Tonto Rim. ■

(ABOVE, LEFT) Payson Junior Rodeo is only one of several of the town's cowboy tournaments.
(ABOVE, CENTER) High-stepping western dancers keep time to fiddle music.
(ABOVE, RIGHT) Calf roping, Junior Rodeo style.
PHOTOS BY NICK BEREZENKO

W H E N   Y O U   G O . . .

Payson boasts a half dozen or more clean, modern, moderately priced hotels. Maybe twice that number of restaurants and cafes compete with fast-food outlets along state routes 87 and 260. Specialty shops cater to visitors, as do several supermarkets, not the least of which is a good-sized Wal-Mart.

For up-to-date information contact:
Payson Chamber of Commerce
State Route 87 at Main Street
P.O. Drawer A

Payson, AZ 85547
(602) 474-4515
The Museum of the Forest
1001 West Main, 85541
(602) 474-3483 (The sign reads Home of Northern Gila County Historical Society Payson Museum.)
Payson Ranger District
Tonto National Forest
U.S. Forest Service
1009 East Highway 260
Payson, AZ 85541
(602) 474-7900
Payson Police Department
303 North Beeline Highway
Payson, AZ 85541

(602) 474-5177
Payson Parks and Recreation
(602) 474-4628

Payson Museum. NICK BEREZENKO

THE SAGA OF LEO THE LION

If Hollywood had scripted it for a fictional movie, critics would have mercilessly panned the plot, to wit:

MGM's Leo the Lion attempts to fly coast to coast.

Crashes in a Payson wilderness.

Lives to roar 10,000 times.

Thanks to cowboys who rescued him.

Plot thins. Totally lacks a love interest.

But this was not a film; rather, a bold quest of publicity. And as such it deserved an Oscar. In fact, the entertainment journal *Variety* dubbed it "the most sensational exploitation stunt ever done in the motion picture industry."

Gruff, cigar-chomping movie mogul Louis B. Mayer complained that things were a little slow at Metro-Goldwyn-Mayer in 1927. America's passion for movies was being overtaken by fascination with flying, popularized by the solo nonstop Atlantic flight of Charles A. Lindbergh.

"Let's fly Leo coast to coast nonstop," suggested publicity director Peter Smith (remember his zany short features, the Pete Smith Specials?).

So over the objections of animal rightists, 350-pound Leo was placed inside a 400-pound steel-and-glass cage encased within the fuselage of a high-wing Ryan Brougham. With barnstormer Martin Jensen at the controls, and the 220-horsepower engine revving over the red line, the monoplane wobbled off an airstrip near San Diego September 16.

Somehow Jensen conquered the Laguna Mountains, traversed the deserts. He refueled in Phoenix and even negotiated a pass in the Mazatzal Mountains. But as he neared the narrowing end of Hells Gate Canyon he realized *no way* did he have the power to climb over the Mogollon Rim dead ahead. So 15 miles east of Payson, with no room to turn around, he stalled the aircraft into a large clump of oak trees, which absorbed most of the energy of the crash. Jenson suffered a cut over his eye. Leo and Leo's cage: miraculously unhurt and intact.

The pilot walked nearly three days southwestward before running onto George Booth near the hamlet of Gisela. When the word got out, the rescue of Leo focused the nation's full attention.

People and equipment mustered at Kohl's Ranch before trucking into Bear Flat. A 15-member party of mostly cowboys went horseback to the crash site, some six straight-line miles, but 12 roundabout. There they found Leo hungry and thirsty, but strong enough inside his cage to be loaded onto a makeshift travois. A skittish team of mules, urged on by Leo's scent and growls, dragged the sled out to the road at Bear Flat. There the cage was loaded onto a truck for transport to Payson.

While regaining his strength, the king of beasts delighted the children of Payson and grabbed headlines around the world.

In time Leo went home. He never flew again, thereby foregoing an untold fortune in frequent flyer credits. ■

Chapter Two

Pine & Strawberry

TWINS AMONG THE TREES

While Payson's connection to The Rim is that of a tidewater town not far from the coast — the ocean is *over there* five leagues — Pine and other small communities beneath The Rim insert themselves right into it, as tiny harbors tucked into a rocky, wave-lashed headland. The Rim is no rumor for the town of Pine. For Pine, The Rim serves as its own enormous shore of a landlocked archipelago. All about, as in Zane Grey's imagery, unbroken woodlands like a verdant, bounding main, extend outward to empty beyond lost horizons.

To a traveler approaching it, The Rim seems slowly to ooze up from the primal basements of the planet, to block out the lower third of the sky. As you draw closer, The Rim asserts itself as sheer towers forming recesses, points, and promontories. Bare rock pokes through the forest in rainbows of warm hues. As often as not, soft white or menacing cobalt clouds decorate a firmament so clear and baby blue it breaks your heart. Eagles in updrafts polish limey brows averaging 7,500 feet above sea level. As the gargantuan hulk leans on the human psyche, time slows to the syncopated clopping of the hooves of a walking cow pony. This is ranching country, lumbering country, relaxing country, wave-through-the-windshield country, unlocked-door country.

After Captain John G. Bourke negotiated the crest of The Rim in 1871, he described it as "a strange freak of nature, a mountain canted up on one side." A hundred ten years later another Arizona author, Charles Bowden, wrote of the Mogollon Rim:

"Here the edge of the great stone wafer to the north slowly erodes backward into itself and spills soil onto the deserts below. The dissolving edge pulsed with periods of uplift, warped with faulting, and wound up higher than either the plateau to the north or the deserts to the south. The lip has

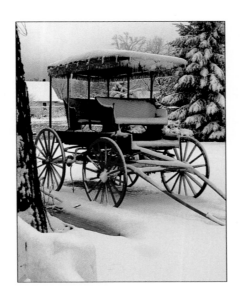

(OPPOSITE PAGE) A tiny enclave clings to a meadow at the edge of the frosty forest at Strawberry.
(RIGHT) Keepsake of a pioneer family, an antique buggy wears wintry decor at Pine. PHOTOS BY NICK BEREZENKO

shed the more recent rock of the geologic clock and is down to Precambrian stone, material a billion or two years old."

From Payson State Route 87 strikes a course northwest and soon tacks down and up the canyon of the East Fork of the Verde River. Enroute to Pine, points of interest worth a look are:

Flowing Spring — Forest Road 272, four miles up State Route 87 from Payson, strikes sharply to the right and down to the East Verde River. About any car can survive the washboard roadbed, to arrive at a concrete ford connecting grassy flats and deciduous arbors on both sides of the river for two miles. Ideal family area with a shallow stream for wading. Except on holiday weekends when you have to pack in your own rock to sit upon, this is a great camping area.

East Verde Park — A quarter mile farther up State Route 87 where the highway crosses the river, FR 622 heads downstream to East Verde Park. Probably more rainbow trout have been caught in this stretch of stream than anywhere else along The Rim. The park ranks as one of the region's favorite picnic spots. And on holidays, ditto the crowds.

Tonto Natural Bridge — Northwest of Payson 9.5 miles, a dead-end graded and graveled road runs three miles west to the bridge. What a surprise David Gowan got in 1877 while prospecting Pine Creek for precious metals. He didn't find his fortune, but he claimed discovery of the world's largest travertine arch. It was newly opened in May 1991 as Tonto Natural Bridge State Park.

Stunning statistics: bridge height, 183 feet; tunnel width, 150 feet; tunnel length, 400 feet. Geologists say it took playful Pine Creek a million years to deposit and sculpt calcium carbonate into today's massive span. During frontier times a five-acre dairy thrived on its top. By some accounts Gowan, a longtime saltwater sailor, initially explored the expansive caverns by swinging himself from side to side on ropes like a pendulum.

Gowan's relatives, in 1927, erected a 10-room lodge. It was once architecturally described as "Staunch American Utilitarian." But the place is homey and, as of this printing, is being refurbished as the visitor center for Arizona's 27th state park. The setting would be charming enough without the bridge: a hidden valley, spring, waterfall, Gowan's early 20th-century fruit trees, and a swimming pool that pioneer Andrew Ogilvie built with a team of four horses pulling a scoop shovel. The park is open every day, and there is an admission charge.

Pine was settled in 1879 by disciples of the Church of Jesus Christ of Latter-day Saints. The Mormon influence remains much in evidence — a tidy church and community center rather typical of western Mormon towns. Today descendants of founders share space with retirees,

(LEFT) Newly constructed overlooks provide fresh views of Arizona's newest state park: Tonto Natural Bridge.
WESLEY HOLDEN
(OPPOSITE PAGE, TOP) Pools, grottoes, and racing rapids grace the landscape near Second Crossing on the East Verde River.
PATRICK FISCHER
(OPPOSITE PAGE, FAR RIGHT) Soaking up the rays and soaking the bodies near Flowing Springs on the East Verde.
WESLEY HOLDEN
(OPPOSITE PAGE, RIGHT) State park staff occupy the historic Tonto Natural Bridge Lodge.
TOM BEAN

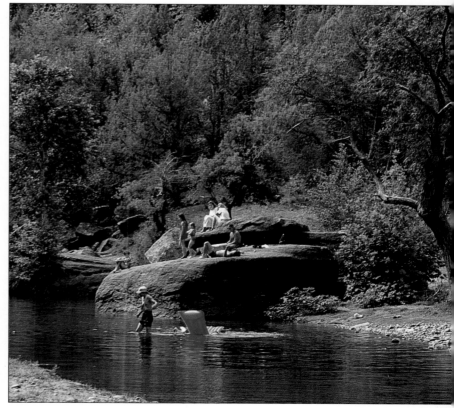

summer home refugees, and spirited young people. Some two-dozen subdivisions tucked off among the pines and junipers bear names like Berry Hill, Eagle Glen, and Canyon Shadows.

Along the main street and by woodsy lanes with casual fence lines, Pine stitches together a loose scatter of antique shops, old farm homes, specialty stores, and service establishments. Here and there a stone or log hut dating to the early days is entrapped within a larger, more modern house.

Following a wet spring, yards bloom with another era's flowers: hollyhocks, asters, and daisies. When Pine stages its down-home Northern Gila County Fair in September, exhibits vary from beef jerky to needlework, wild grape jam, sunbonnets, bola ties, and Big Max pumpkins. The fair is but one of a dozen area festivals staged during the warmer months.

The Pine/Strawberry Museum is located in the old school office building in Pine. The 10 display cases holding pioneer artifacts, handsome enough

in their own right, are the more appreciated for having been locally made by Leroy Horton while seated in a wheelchair. Available here is the booklet, "A Walking History Trail of Pine and Strawberry." They also have it at the local Chamber of Commerce.

In common with the rest of The Rim Country, Pine's climate challenges prediction. At 5,400 feet, Pine perches 400 feet higher than Payson. In early spring and late fall that's enough to turn Payson drizzle into Pine sleet. And one May Day you could savor the chef's special in The Rim Cafe while a brisk snow shower slants past the windows. Deep snowpacks some years persist atop The Rim while the first catch of squash and beans sprouts in Pine's backyard patches.

"We can follow the seasons by what falls on our heads," says Artist Bill Ahrendt. "One month the pine needles descend, and another brings a rain of tiny worms. The oaks lose their leaves in the spring, and there are times when there's so much pollen, it coats everything like volcanic ash.

"And smells. You can close your eyes and still perceive the doings of Mother Nature. On a nice warm day when the sap is running, you can go up to one of those old ponderosa pines, put your arms around it and bury your nose in one of those yellow streaks in the bark, and inhale the most delicious fragrance of sugary butterscotch. Yes, butterscotch."

A distinguished teacher as well as draftsman and painter, Ahrendt adjudges The Rim's residents and visitors to have an artistic streak: "We don't qualify as a colony, but there are enough enclaves of artists, artisans, and patrons to lend a measure of culture to our communities." To prove the point: Annual arts and crafts events customarily bring together from 30 to 50 Rim Country artists and artisans, running the gamut from classical egg tempera painting to keen custom knife-making.

Of birds: An internationally known artist, Larry Toschick, who for 16 years painted wildlife at his home near Pine, counted 45 species of birds on his lot. Now for health reasons a desert dweller, Larry pines for Pine, "and its incredibly rich variety of species. The raptors are wonderful: Cooper's, sharp-shinned and sparrow hawks, as well as the common red-tailed. You'll see flocks of band-tail pigeon, choirs of several kinds of warblers together, and pairs of sandhill cranes. They are God's gifts."

Strawberry, the hamlet and valley, lie 3 miles northwest of Pine. At 6,800 feet, another notch up the climatological ladder, Strawberry can copy Maine while Payson feels like Mexico. Strawberry measured six feet of snow on the level in December 1967 and four feet in two days in February 1986. But some winters, snowfall is light.

Pride of Strawberry is The Schoolhouse. It's 1.6 miles west of State Route 87 on the Fossil Creek Road. To be fair to all, the site was selected in the exact center of Strawberry Valley. Built in 1885 of huge, squared pine logs, the structure is the oldest standing schoolhouse in Arizona. Today it is restored and equipped in original condition, testifying to the yearning for education on the raw frontier. Only one room, it was elegant for its time, with paneled wainscotting and wallpaper. The Strawberry Schoolhouse is open and staffed for visitation during the summer season.

Within its gently sloping swales, Strawberry tends hobby farms and orchards, pens pet horses, and trades in real estate. Out on the highway, little businesses like Lonnie's Enchanted Cottage cater to tourists. Breakfast at the Strawberry Lodge continues a tradition older than granite. Sportsman's Chalet across the street boasts of the only elevator in town — a dumb waiter that lifts drinks to the pool shooters on the second floor.

If trails were freeways, the Pine-Strawberry area would make a world-class interchange. Hiker's heaven. Options galore. At the Pine Trailhead at the south end of Pine take your pick from the Pine Canyon Trail, Donahue Trail, Oak Springs Trail, and best known, the old Highline Trail (see map on pages 32-33).

Hugging the base of The Rim from Pine to State Route 260 east of Christopher Creek, the Highline long served pioneers as a transportation and commercial link across this rugged land. You can hike, horseback, or mountain bike the Highline's 51-mile

entirety, camping along the way. Or, since roads cross it at convenient intervals, it can be divided into day hikes. Located at about 5,500 feet elevation, the Highline is a year-round trail only occasionally closed by snow. Vegetation along the route ranges from cactus and manzanita to piñon and juniper to ponderosa pine and fir. The trail crosses a number of perennial streams and offers spectacular views of the Rim above and the basins and ranges below.

For back country explorers, perhaps the greater harm inflicted by the Dude Fire of 1990 was the charring of the very heart of the Highline. Until the Dude, the Highline was vegetated for nearly all of its 51 miles along the base of The Rim's cliffs. The fire took out the 17-mile central section of trail from Dude Creek to the Tonto Fish Hatchery. The Highline is still walkable end to end — and deer, elk, and other wildlife thrive on the new grasses — but that central section will take a century and more to regain its before-the-fire appearance.

(OPPOSITE PAGE) "Out to feed the horses," South Road, Pine.
NICK BEREZENKO
(ABOVE) Readin', writin', 'rithmetic and restoration at the Strawberry Schoolhouse.
BOB AND SUZANNE CLEMENZ
(LEFT) Ralph Fuller and Bill Barcus run a batch of apple cider through a relic press.
NICK BEREZENKO

Lichens now stain the floor of an ancient ocean: Limestone overhanging the village of Pine at Fuller Point.
NICK BEREZENKO

But if something less strenuous is your style, the unfailing thrill of Strawberry is driving the ascent/descent of State Route 87 between the lodge and The Rim. On top more than one traveler has likened the stunning panorama of Strawberry Valley, to "standing on the edge of the earth." That is where, incidentally, a certain school bus almost sailed off long, long ago.

You can double back (take it easy!) through Pine and about two miles south to an unpaved gravel track wending eastward. Its name: The Control Road (FR 64).

There, at the Control Road/State Route 87 intersection, sprawls an excellent hunting ground for fossils of shellfish and other denizens of the deep — evidence that these mile-high mounts once formed the bottom of a sea. Rockhounds consider The Rim country to be a mineralogist's dream-come-true. Chert, quartz, and gem-quality geodes are plentiful. Just about any prospector or rock shop can put you onto a scatter of handsome red jasper or agate.

The Control Road, constructed by the Forest Service to assist suppression of wildfire, is not designed for a fast pace. It bends through slopes bristling with cactus patches and spear-shaped succulents, ferns and forbs, through prime specimens of what botanists call the Transition Zone: that contour of climate neither arid nor alpine, a land of thrifty piñon pines and alligator juniper, of stubborn barberry bush and fine-leaf yucca, perennial bunchgrass and annual wildflowers, of gnarled manzanita and Emery oak. Along this road, numerous shaded nooks provide room for movable feasts. Ever hanging overhead to the north is Milk Ranch Point, a six-square-mile mesa that would be a "sky island" were it not for a narrow causeway connecting it to The Rim. Long ago it took its name from the dairy on its top.

The Control Road crosses numerous live and intermittent watercourses in its 10 miles before intercepting FR 199 south of the summer home community of Washington Park. You can push on eastward 14 miles to where the Control Road joins State Route 260 near Kohl's Ranch on Tonto Creek. Or you can take 199 south, a 13-mile loop back to Payson via the Houston Mesa Road, one of the loveliest drives of The Rim Country.

FR 199 visits rustic homes with shaded yards, gardens by orchards, and stone walls encircling weathered barns. It also crosses the gushing East Verde three times over concrete fords.

About two miles down FR 199 a ridge falls away

to present a grand panorama of the Mazatzal Wilderness filling the horizon. As the Indian chief said: "In the end, there is only the sky and the mountain."

Seven and a half miles south on 199 to the east sprawls Sunflower Mesa and the Shoofly Prehistoric Ruin. "Arizona to an archaeologist is what the Pacific Ocean is to Jacques Cousteau," a journalist once wrote. "It's the best." It was in Arizona that incontrovertible evidence placed elephant hunters in America more than 10,000 years ago. Many of Arizona's federal, state, and local parks protect and interpret prehistoric sites. And Arizona digs in progress are pushing the time of the first Americans back to 30,000 years before present.

Not nearly so old, but no less compelling, is the Shoofly site to the east of the Houston Mesa summer home community. Shoofly (named for nearby Shoofly Canyon) was extensively investigated by archaeologists from Arizona State University during summers of the mid-1980s.

Deduction and laboratory analysis of a wealth of artifacts and material, in a scholarly sense, brought Shoofly Town back to life. Gaining dates from tree rings in building timbers and from radiocarbon measurement, scientists concluded that Shoofly was occupied as early as A.D. 550 and peaked as an 80-house village about A.D. 1100. These were a cosmopolitan people, perhaps at most 60 families, and of mysterious customs. Over time they built at least three types of houses, such as ovals and squares. Few individuals grew much taller than five feet. They raised corn, squash, and beans and hunted deer and rabbit. They domesticated the dog and turkey. They fired a plain brown pottery and crafted jewelry of shell. Shoofly residents, in a most unusual project, surrounded their six-acre neighborhood with a thick, low stone wall. Although life expectancy was grimly short, the village endured — until the early 1300s, when for reasons unknown, the people throughout the region disappeared.

A wealth of knowledge about these "Payson People" emerged from the digs, but enigmas remained. Why, in a chamber, did the people have 40 deer jaws decorated with turquoise? Why did they bind the heads of their children to deform their skulls? Why were the customs at Shoofly radically different from people who lived in surrounding suburbs? Shoofly's principal investigator could only say, "They were their own people."

You may visit Shoofly, but remember that laws forbid collecting and molesting anything. Leave nothing but footprints, take nothing but photographs and memories. From Shoofly the drive back to Payson is only a few miles, but...in time...from Shoofly to Payson it's a thousand years. ■

W H E N   Y O U   G O . . .

Lodges and cabin courts put up guests in Pine and Strawberry, and there are several small- to modest-sized restaurants. Guided horseback trail ride outfitters operate in the area during the warmer seasons. Trail information is available from the forest headquarters listed below.

Chamber of Commerce
P.O. Box 196, Pine, AZ 85544
(602) 476-3547
Tonto National Forest
2324 East McDowell Road
Phoenix, AZ 85006

(602) 225-5200
Tonto National Forest
Payson Ranger District
1009 East Highway 260
Payson, AZ 85541
(602) 474-7900
Arizona Mineral Museum
1502 W. Washington
Phoenix, AZ 85007
(602) 255-3791
Arizona State Parks, and the
Historic Preservation Office
of Arizona State Parks
800 W. Washington, Suite 415
Phoenix, AZ 85007
(602) 542-4174

Pine Canyon trail. NICK BEREZENKO

Chapter Three

East of Payson four miles through the pines on State Route 260, a once-vacant ranch meadow is now an eclectic cluster of commercial enterprises. The name: Star Valley. Pat Cline holds the preeminent right to comment upon happenings in the valley, for in the yard of her longtime home is buried Old Man Starr (two Rs), the pioneer for whom the place is named. Starr was killed in a freighting wreck, and the Houston brothers buried him "inside the fence of the cienega so that animals couldn't walk on him." Mrs. (Raymond) Cline is a third generation Haught. One of the first generation in The Rim Country, S.A. Haught, once told a newspaper feature writer how he got to The Rim:

"I started out May 1, 1885, for Arizona from a point 15 miles east of Dallas City, and was driving 115 head of cattle. The Texas Panhandle had a quarantine on cattle south of the Texas and Pacific Railroad and I went through Indian Territory, thence through no man's land to New Mexico, crossed the Rio Grande River at Albuquerque, then to Holbrook and Tonto Basin. It was 450 miles out of my way...but I never lost a cow."

CIRCUM-NAVIGATING Diamond Point

It says something about the tenacity of the Haught strain that more than a hundred years later S.A. had three sons living — one sired when he was in his 70s.

When Pat was a young woman today's State Route 260 through Star Valley was a gravel road just wagon-wide with occasional turnouts for passing. Recently, as a highway construction flag woman, Pat stood with her arms akimbo and shook her head at something big going on.

"Civilization has arrived," she said, "when they put concrete sidewalks along the road

(LEFT) This young bull is one of a burgeoning population of Rocky Mountain elk. This species was transplanted long ago from Yellowstone to take the place of extinct Merriam's elk. WILLIAM E. BARKUS
(RIGHT) Pat and Raymond Cline show off a pair of family branding irons at their older-than-a-century homesite in Star Valley. NICK BEREZENKO

through Star Valley."

It is true. In a monumental work, State Route 260 below The Rim has become more freeway than lane; the main artery of The Rim Country speeds travelers across the northern portion of the land below The Rim. Trips that used to take days now can be done in minutes.

All that said, you have to wonder what those folks three and four generations ago would make of Star Valley and its sidewalks now. And of the nearby BZB Nursery operated by Marvin Isbell.

Isbell probably knows more than anybody about gardening the Southwest between 5,000 and 6,000 feet — a broad contour of problem soils, killer winds, insect plagues, and two months (May and June) that often can go straight through with scarcely a drop of rain. The Rim Country also can experience

standbys — corn, squash, beans — bolt past July into September, with a bonus for a recreational gardener: They grew in The Rim Country thousands of years before Columbus. Other consistent winners: green onions, string beans, tomatoes, peppers, and berries.

Roses love warm seasons in The Rim Country, but require winter protection. Long ago some pioneer woman brought a darkly hued domestic iris bulb and today it is everywhere, nicknamed Payson Purple. Here's a little list of other flowers that do well in The Rim's realm: cosmos, zinnias, hollyhocks, and forsythia.

Call it human nature, but perhaps it is through plants and animals that we relate to a national forest. The primary tree associated with The Rim Country is the ponderosa pine. It rises up out of

rience a mild winter, a balmy, moist spring, an idyllic summer, and an autumn that pours a cornucopia of vegetables and fruit into Rim kitchens and roadside produce stands.

But don't count on it. "Just when you think you have it figured out," says Isbell, "January comes in April, and August extends into October. Or the

grasshoppers explode, or the javelinas raid, or the elk dismantle the elk-proof fences. It helps to keep in mind that even in the mountains we're still within a semi-arid state. Spells of low humidity are as much to be feared as late and early frosts."

So much for accentuating the negative. Orchards of apples and peaches and apricots some years droop with limbloads of luscious bounty. Those Southwestern

the ground, gestures grandly, and tosses its hair. It provides oxygen, shade, food, shelter, habitat, even music. Yes, as John Muir declared of the ponderosa, "Of all pines, this one gives forth the finest music to the winds." Photographer and author Jim Tallon adds: "More than a thousand species of wildlife are interrelated with — and, in some cases, dependent upon — the ponderosa pine."

For a trip through this ponderosa pine forest and more, you're offered a loop that takes State Route 260 from Payson, past Star Valley to the east end of the Control Road, then circles back west and south for a return to Payson. Often in view out the left-hand window looms 6,384-foot Diamond Point, under The Rim a minor but strategically located rise from which much fire-endangered forest can be seen. Diamond Point got its name from fields of quartz crystals that litter the area.

It was from FR 64, 15.2 miles east of Payson, that the defense was mounted against what is called the

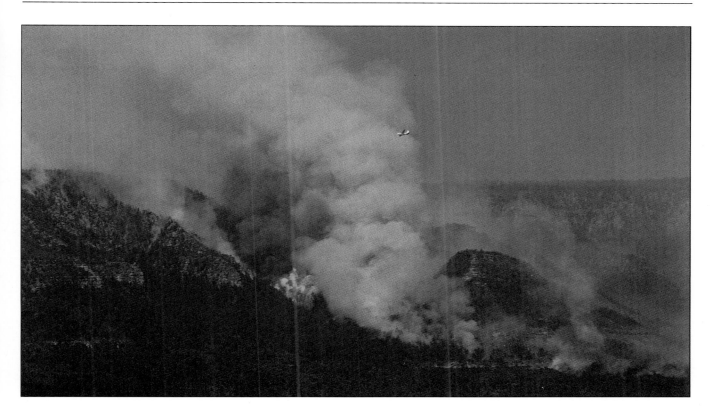

(ABOVE) An aerial tanker zooms in to drop fire-retardant slurry onto the Dude Fire, June, 1990. NICK BEREZENKO
(OPPOSITE PAGE, LEFT TO RIGHT) Wild iris, Indian paintbrush, columbine, wild Arizona rose. STEWART AITCHISON
(OPPOSITE PAGE, BELOW) His green thumb reaching to the elbow, Marvin Isbell pinches back tea roses at his BZB Nursery, two miles east of Star Valley off Dealer's Choice Road. NICK BEREZENKO

worst fire in Arizona's history. The Control Road passes through several burned-over miles and affords access to the Dude Fire Auto Tour. On the way the road passes clusters of summer homes and crosses several trout streams such as Bonita and Ellison creeks, the latter named for the father of Miss Duette Ellison.

The Ellisons founded the Apple Ranch, so named for its 3,000 fruit trees. Located as it was on a main east-west trail, the Apple Ranch served as a way station for travelers through the 1880s and '90s. Miss Duette, a vivacious and musically talented ranch girl, married governor-to-be George W.P. Hunt to become Arizona's *first*, first lady.

But regarding the Dude fire. On a dry, windy day in late June 1990, lightning ignited a fire in the Dude Creek drainage 12 miles northeast of Payson. For a week the conflagration roared across the face of The Rim, eventually costing the lives of six fire-fighters, blackening 24,174 acres of mostly Tonto National Forest, destroying 51 cabins, chasing a thousand people from their homes, and doing $12 million in damage. The holocaust took out a swath three miles wide and 14 miles long, and by insidious selection, burned down Zane Grey's cabin and, nearby, the equally historic Babe Haught log house.

The FR 29 turnoff to the Dude Fire Auto Tour is 4.2 miles west of State Route 260. (The Payson Ranger Station offers a free informative brochure "The Story of the Dude Burn.")

Soon you come upon the numbered posts:

1. This is what the forest looked like before the burn.

2. The Rim dead ahead, so huge it can create its own weather.

3. A place where the fire was fought with bull-dozed fire lines and aerial bombardment with chemical retardant.

4. A badly burned place, reseeded with soil-holding plants.

5. Thoroughly charred, it will be generations before the forest returns. But much is sprouting.

6. Same fire, different results. On one side of the road the fire burned incredibly hot, actually boiling and exploding sap. Across the road the fire took away ground fuel, and left many trees untouched.

7. An erosion control structure.

8. Only blackened sticks remain.

The relatively unpopulated grandeur of Tonto National Forest, as seen from Diamond Point, southward over Star Valley to the distant Mazatzal Wilderness. NICK BEREZENKO

9. Lushly growing ground cover, some from the 250,000 pounds of seed broadcast via helicopters immediately after the fire.

10. Private land, where luckily no homes were destroyed.

The last two Stations, 11 and 12, can be reached only by high-clearance vehicles, preferably with four-wheel drive. Number 11 marks the old Roberts Burn of 1961, which is returning to forest. The twelfth post is at Big Canyon where nature is healing itself after severe erosion. In all, the motoring tour extends seven miles.

"It's like springtime every day out there," observed a Payson Ranger. He explained that before occupation by whites, the forest burned periodically — set afire by lightning or the Indians. Because of the fires' frequency, fuel for hot disastrous blazes did not accumulate. A century of unnatural fire suppression allowed forest debris to pile up and carry fire into treetops. Now the Dude is experiencing its own "sweet season of renewal." With the help of its friends, long-range programs of reforestation, stream protection, fisheries revival, trail stabilization, and wildlife assistance are progressing. In time, this blackened portion of the Tonto will be more gorgeous than before the Dude fire.

Back on the Control Road, just a tenth of a mile past FR 29, FR 65 leads you four miles to Diamond Point Lookout. The views from the point are sensational, and in summer, you'll find other visitors to Diamond Point — swarms of colorful ladybugs.

From the Dude tour, the Control Road progresses through groves of ancient alligator juniper, dry washes, and green forest for 4.5 miles, to enter the southern portion of the Dude Burn. Then for nearly three miles you drive through burnscape, which likewise is on the mend. Two miles more and you join FR 199. Turn south and you will return 13 miles to Payson.

And ever on your left looms the landmark Diamond Point. ■

WHEN YOU GO...

This portion of The Rim country lies within the Payson Ranger District of Tonto National Forest. The ranger station is at 1009 East Highway 260, Payson, AZ 85541, telephone (602) 474-7900. Maps, brochures, and chummy advice are readily available. Particularly well done are:

"Payson Ranger District Discovery Tour," free four-page guide.

"The Story of the Dude Fire," free brochure.

Tonto National Forest Map, standard fee.

For graphic insights into the sorry lot and laborious life of a turn-of-the-century ranch wife, read Marguerite Noble's classic novel *Filaree*, first published in 1979 by Random House. Still going strong after numerous domestic and foreign editions, the latest printing is by the University of New Mexico Press: Albuquerque, 1986.

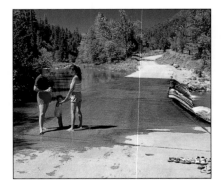

Hard to believe this placid trickle of Tonto Creek at the Bear Flat crossing can be transformed into a torrent when the heavens open over the Mogollon. NICK BEREZENKO

DON'T EVEN THINK ABOUT DOING IT

One March a warm rain fell on the snow pack. Of a late morning we inched our way down the slippery, eroded road to Bear Flat. We wanted to watch Tonto Creek roll boulders and toss tree trunks. We were not disappointed. The normally placid ford over to the summer homes was transformed into a violent sluice. Presently, a most improbable figure appeared on the eastern shore: a young man covered by mud.

"I need a pull," he cried.

Well, you'd almost have to own a four-wheeler to understand how difficult it can be to turn down a sincere plea for a rescue. It's sort of a priestly calling.

I had been across the ford dozens of times, and I thought I knew the bottom. So with little dawdling, I launched my hoopie into the maelstrom. Deeper than I thought! And whoops! in midstream the bottom was gone — all the way to Hells Gate, likely. Then the engine upped and died.

Tonto heaved its strength against the left side of the little Jeep, which now and then would give a bit of ground toward the churning rapids downstream. It dawned on me that I was either going to save my life by saving the Jeep, or probably lose them both.

Yes, luck. In the back were a couple of dry rags and a toolbox. I fetched a wrench, climbed out around the windshield, stood on a flat fender, and threw back the hood. Water propelled by the radiator fan had drenched the spark plugs and distributor. I dried them best I could. The Jeep jumped downstream a couple of feet. Quickly I reached underwater, loosened the generator bracket with the wrench, and removed the fan belt from the pulley.

Flopped the hood shut. Swung around the windshield. Hit the ignition. Vaaaaa-roooom! Jeep and I roared out of the water pocket and made the other side.

In the recklessness of youth I pulled the fellow's sedan out of a bog, dropped my tow bar onto his trailer hitch, removed his fan belt, and plunged into Tonto a second time. We aimed in tandem as high upstream as physics allowed, and we emerged within inches of missing the downstream exit. We clawed to safety like a mechanical alligator.

Then we opened some cans and laughed so long and hard that tears streaked from our faces and splashed onto trembling hands.

If not too low-slung, most cars in good condition can make it if FR 405 isn't wet or cut by rain. FR 405 departs the south side of State Route 260 at the Thompson Draw Summer Homes Unit I turnoff, 14.4 miles east of Payson. To Bear Flat is about seven miles, and the last four-mile stretch is a pistol: 24 percent grades, washboard surface and throat-grabbing overviews. You must take the outer lane descending, but soothe your nerves in the knowledge that you get the inner lane returning.

At the flat is a small but handsome camping area, a massive concrete apron, and access to favorite stocked fishing holes. Even with the newer apron, I would not launch an atomic submarine into the flooded Tonto, let alone a car. That applies to you, too. Don't even *think* about doing it! ■

COCONINO NATIONAL FOREST

West Clear Creek

WEST CLEAR CREEK WILDERNESS

Calloway Lake

To Camp Verde →

FOSSIL SPRINGS WILDERNESS

FR 81

FR 81E

To Flagstaff

FH 3

FR 211

FR 8IE

General Crook Trail

MOGOLLON PLATEAU

FR 147

East Clear Creek

FR 141

Clints Well Campground ▲

Clints Well

87

FR 138

Blue Ridge Campground ▲

Blue Ridge Ranger Station

To Winslow

Rock Crossing Campground ▲

FR 751

Creek

Blue Ridge Reservoir

FR 95

Coconino Nat. For.

Apache-Sitgreaves Nat. For.

Battleground Ridge Fight FR 123E

FR 123

FR 95

Pinchot Springs Cabin

FR 96

FR 300

Kehl Campground ▲

Crackerbox Canyon

General Springs Cabin ▲

Battle of Big Dry Wash Monument

Barbershop Canyon

FR 137

Buck Springs Cabin ▲

Knoll Lake Campground ▲

260

87

FR 218A

Baker Butte ◉

Milk Ranch Point

FR 218

Bray Burn
June, 1990 — 497 acres

Washington Park

FR 295E

Knoll Lake

Bear Canyon Lake

Strawberry Schoolhouse

Pine Canyon Trail

Highline Trail

FR 708

87

STRAWBERRY

Strawberry Valley

FR 428

PINE

Donahue Trail

Highline Trail

Oak Springs Trail

FR 32

FR 199

Verde Glen ▲

Gila County

Coconino County

FR 300

Highline Trail

Highline Trail

Zane Grey Lodge site

Fish Hatchery

FR 300

FR 8

TONTO NATIONAL FOREST

Highline Trail

FR 64

Third Crossing

Second Crossing ▲

Water Wheel

First Crossing

Ellison

Myrtle Point

Dude Burn
June, 1990 — 28,480 acres

Creek

FR 289

Tonto Creek Campground ▲

Upper Tonto Creek Campground ▲

Promontory Butte

MAZATZAL WILDERNESS

FR 583

Tonto Natural Bridge State Park

Webber Creek

River

FR 272

Flowing Spring ▲

Diamond Rim

FR 65

Tonto Village

FR 64

Kohl's Ranch

260

Chris

Camp Tontozona

FR 405

MAZATZAL WILDERNESS

Verde

FR 622

East Verde

Pine Creek

87

Payson Airport ☐

FR 406

PAYSON

Diamond Point Lookout ◉

260

Star Valley

Payson Ranger Station

☐ Tonto Apache Ind. Res.

To Phoenix ↓

Ponderosa Campground ▲

Bear Flat

Christophe Creek Campgroun ▲

Tonto Creek

HELLSGATE WILDERNESS

Mazatzal Mtns.

The Mogollon Rim Country, land for all seasons: In spring canoes cruise the clear waters of Rim lakes.

Summer brings hikes along the gurgling streams that flow from beneath The Rim.

PHOTOGRAPHS BY NICK BEREZENKO

Arizona

To Winslow

Chevelon
Ranger Station

LEGEND

Paved Road		Private Land	
All Weather Graded Road		Wilderness Area	
Light Duty Road		Recent Forest Burns	
Four-wheel-drive Road		Lakes and Streams	
Hiking Trail		Settlements	
National Forest (above the rim)		Places of Interest	
National Forest (below the rim)		Campground	
Indian Reservation		Dispersed Camping	
Ranger Station		Fire Lookout	

Scale in Miles
0   5   10

Chevelon
Crossing
Campground

Chevelon Creek

FR 169

Chevelon
Canyon Lake

FR 169B

Weimer
Point

FR 90   FR 170

FR 34

FR 100

FR 504

COLORADO PLATEAU

To Holbrook

FR 99

277

260

HEBER

OVERGAARD

Heber
Ranger
Station

To Show Low

FR 144

FR 51   260

FR 146

APACHE-SITGREAVES   NATIONAL FOREST

FR 169

*Canyon
ke*

MOGOLLON MESA

*Woods
Canyon Lake*

FR 195

pen

Spillway
Campground

*Willow Springs
Lake*

ollon   Crook   Rim

FR 149

FR 291

Al Fulton Point

FR 171

Colcord

Colcord

FR 512

FR 33

FR 34

FR 188

Naegelin Rim

To Young

Coconino County
Navajo County

FR 99

Forest Lakes

Sink Hole
Campground

Canyon Point
Campground

FR 86

Black Canyon Lake

Pleasant Valley War Graves

Gentry
Campground

Black Canyon Rim
Campground

Fish Hatchery

Canyon
Creek

Airplane
Flat

Valentine Ridge
Campground

Gila County
Navajo County

Old Verde Road

General Crook Trail

FR 300

Mogollon Rim

FR 124

FR 166

Phoenix
Park

Bear Springs

FR 125

**FORT APACHE
INDIAN RESERVATION**

TONTO NATIONAL FOREST

Recreational travel on the
Fort Apache Indian Reservation
requires a permit in advance.
Write: Fort Apache Game and Fish,
P.O. Box 220, Whiteriver, AZ 85941

Autumn invites
leisurely rambles
among the quaking
asspens.
JAMES TALLON

Winter beckons the
cross-country skier to
explore the pristine
countryside.
C. BRIAN BECK

Chapter Four

Kohl's Ranch, perched on the west bank of Tonto Creek, is not so much a ranch as a village complete with a lovely hotel, restaurant, and summer homes. Kohl's put up guests free when it was a cow ranch in the 1880s, then new owners began charging for bed and board in 1927. As late as the 1950s a tiny tavern boasted of seven stools and one curvaceous Coca-Cola glass, "If," as the aromatic, grizzly, toothless bartender was fond of saying, "a lady ever stops by, but so far, she hain't." Women were so scarce for all-night dances, men had to dance with brooms while waiting for the chance to cut in. Now lots of ladies stop by.

In addition to the fishing, camping, hunting, horseback riding, and hosting in and around Kohl's, across the creek beckons the Open Air Chapel where local pastors conduct nondenominational services on summerish Sabbaths. Down the Tonto from Kohl's sprawls Camp Tontozona where, during training dates in late summer, visitors are welcome to witness the football geniuses of Arizona State University whip young Sun Devils into shape. Large public campgrounds bracket Kohl's Ranch, with some camp-

Tonto Creek
WHERE LIFE QUICKENS

sites big enough for trailers and motor homes.

There used to be two outstanding destinations in the Kohl's Ranch area. Now one is gone. On June 27, 1990, the Dude Fire destroyed the cabin where Zane Grey chose to spend much of his time in the 'teens and '20s of this century. Where he wrote Western novels — often in 30 days of intense scribbling. Where he based his hunts after bear, lion, and deer. And where in 1929 he brought a group of friends and planned a big hunting party out of season. Arizona would not allow it, and Grey threw a fit. Arizona owed him for the publicity he brought to it, he fumed. Grey vowed to leave the state forever...and did.

For three decades the cabin

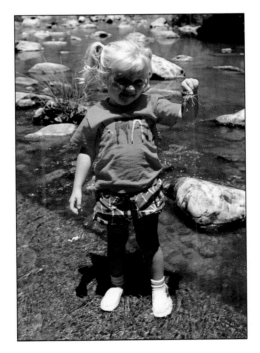

(OPPOSITE PAGE) Deciduous trees such as black walnut, oak, and box elder commingle with conifers along Tonto Creek near Kohl's Ranch. By summer's end, wild grapevines drape trees as high as 40 feet.
JERRY JACKA
(RIGHT) Before slipping it back into the water, a young fisherwoman, shows off her Tonto Creek crayfish.
NICK BEREZENKO

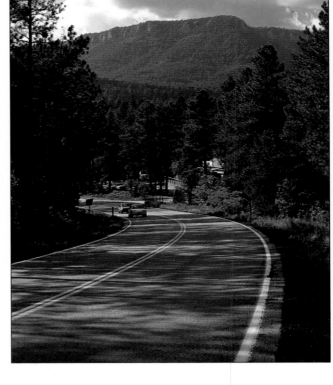

deteriorated until it caught the attention of Phoenix air-conditioning magnate William Goettl (rhymes with metal). Goettl purchased the property from the Grey family in 1962, and he and his crew restored the cabin to its original status. It was opened for the enjoyment and education of the public and in 1974 was included in the National Register of Historic Places.

On a happier note, the state's Tonto Fish Hatchery was saved by a brave and determined crew of fire-fighters in the same day that the adjacent Grey cabin burned. The hatchery holds a special, sentimental place in the author's psyche, as one of his first trout treks 40 years before:

Now the tiny, ex-World War II Jeep in four-wheel drive slogs through the frost-heaved decomposed granite of the steeply pitched forest path, climbing from an elevation of 5,600 to 6,400 feet in a reach of about four miles.

The thin conifer-perfumed late-March air pours through the doorless 4X4 and pierces my quilted parka. Patches of snow blanket the north-facing slopes. Along the way, I am startled by a herd of pregnant mule deer does and delighted by gray squirrels busily trying to recall where they hid last fall's acorns.

At last can be seen a rustic gate, which I take to be the end of the trail. The heavy snow pack under and beyond the Mogollon Rim has not yet melted, but Tonto Creek is running a fair head of water. With numbed fingers I fiddle with rod and reel, line, and leader....

Fluffy, moist snow-flakes begin to flutter down through the hard-woods, almost making me decide to hike my cold feet to the Jeep and retreat. But in a short walk upstream I come to a fence beyond which lurks a huge, quiet, bramble-free pool. The fence is not much of a barrier — just a few strands of wire through which a bull elk might amble.

There, even an amateur fly-caster should luck out. And that I do. On the first presentation of an artificial larva, the surface of the pond erupts with

(ABOVE, LEFT) Campfire and lantern illuminate a cozy bivouac at Christopher Creek Campground. Nearby rises Christopher Mountain, a dandy expanse for hunting during deer season. NICK BEREZENKO (ABOVE, RIGHT) Cabins, cafes, and other roadside facilities including RV and mobile home parks come together at Christopher Creek, five miles east of Kohl's Ranch on State Route 260. NICK BEREZENKO (OPPOSITE PAGE) Somewhere in the vicinity of serene Christopher Creek, goes a legend, is buried the fortune of the first settler, Isadore Christopher. P.K. WEIS

a primeval force. Then the fish feels the hook and sounds. The line seems anchored to the bottom. Then I sense a bit of give, gain a few feet and gently play the lunker near to the shore. With a swish of net, the great rainbow, fat with roe, maybe 15, 16 inches long, is mine.... With every cast, there rises a monster trout.

When I am done, I dismantle my gear and pack the fish into my creel. They overfill it, and I must tote a few on a string. Then I notice a humble road lying a few hundred feet to the west. Why fight my way through the thickets? I climb onto a piece of meadow and stroll down the road toward the Jeep. At the gate is posted a hand-crafted sign: "Hope you enjoyed your visit to the Tonto Fish Hatchery." I have been fishing in a brood pond! I skulk back into the woods, stow the gear and plunder in the hoopie, smear some mud on my license plate, and light a shuck for home.

Thank the Lord for statutes of limitations. Even I am welcome there, and you, too, if you leave your fishing gear in your car.

The hatchery is open seven days a week, 8 a.m. to 5 p.m., from late spring to autumn. Self-guided tours and a visitor center will inform you that whereas a natural trout stream can produce only about 225 catchable fish per mile, per year, the Tonto hatchery produces 180,000 in the same period. From egg to nine-incher takes about a year. About 2,500 fish are distributed into Tonto, Christopher, and Verde drainages on a normal weekend. The stocking is doubled for holidays.

"...The source of Tonto Creek is itself a special phenomenon," writes my friend George Collins. "It flows at the rate of 1,500 gallons per minute; the headwaters maintain a constant temperature of 48 degrees. Established in 1936, the hatchery is an absorbingly interesting place, educational and useful, worth far more than it costs."

It's sad to leave such havens. But more places of interest, such as Christopher Creek, summon you on. Local chronicler Peggy Benz offers a bit of history:

"Christopher Creek [the community] is located just 25 miles northeast of Payson on Highway 260 at an elevation of 6,000 feet. Both Christopher Creek and Christopher Mountain were named in honor of an early French settler Isador Christopher.... He lived here with his mail-order bride, Mary. In July 1882 Christopher had killed a bear, skinned it, and hung the skinned bear in one of his cabins. While he was out hunting the next day, Apaches came and burned two of his buildings. And while these buildings were still smoldering, U.S. Army troops came along. They found these animal remains and, thinking the Indians had

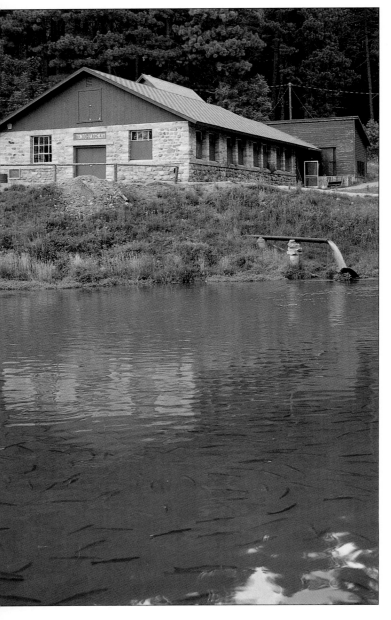

(LEFT) Mature rainbow trout cruise a holding pond below the covered raceways of Tonto Creek Fish Hatchery. Newly upgraded, the hatchery is capable of producing annually a quarter million fish for stocking in Arizona streams. BOB AND SUZANNE CLEMENZ
(OPPOSITE PAGE, TOP) U.S. cavalrymen reverently inter the remains of a skinned bear, in the belief it was Old Man Christopher killed by Indians. SCRATCH BOARD ILLUSTRATION BY BILL AHRENDT

killed Christopher, the troops gave the bear a solemn funeral and burial."

That knowledge ought not to affect your appetite. Several good restaurants prosper at Christopher, including the favorite Creekside Inn. Aside from commercial enterprises, Christopher has large public campgrounds, dependable fishing, and a wonder-filled network of hiking and horse trails.

Then snug down your seat belts. The nine-mile piece of Highway 260 from Christopher to the top of The Rim is a marvelous but contentious marriage between road engineers and Mother Nature. With Promontory Butte and like land masses darkening the north, the modern tarmac bends and climbs past the Two-sixty Trailhead (eastern terminus of the Highline Trail) and at times soars heavenward so sharply your automobile will seem like a flying

machine in takeoff. Southward — four, five, six, seven blue-gray ridges come into view, and by the time you reach the top at Al Fulton Point, the feeling of flight almost becomes real. It's as though you are floating above a painting by Maynard Dixon, or Ed Mell.

No better spot for contemplating nature. It calls to mind the preachings of early naturalists.

Thoreau: "This curious world we inhabit is more wonderful than convenient; more beautiful than it is useful; it is more to be admired and enjoyed than used."

Muir: "Climb the mountains and get their good tidings. Nature's peace will flow into you as sunshine flows into trees. The winds will blow their own freshness into you and the storms their energy, while cares will drop off like autumn leaves." ∎

W H E N   Y O U   G O . . .

Facilities for this section under The Rim are concentrated at old homestead land now in private hands, mainly but not limited to Star Valley, Kohl's Ranch, and Christopher Creek. Food, fuel, and lodgings are available at all three places.

Tonto Fish Hatchery, is at the end of FR 289 four miles north from State Route 260, (602) 478-4200.

From the Forest Service office in Payson or Overgaard obtain an "On Your Own in Southwestern Mountains" brochure, and "Leave 'No Trace' Land Ethics" guidebook. Both are free and chockablock full of guidance for outback exploration.

Numerous stables under and atop the Mogollon Rim rent saddle horses for exploring backcountry tracks dating to frontier times. Here a trio traverses the Highline Trail near Horton Creek.
NICK BEREZENKO

IN QUEST OF THE GHOST OF HORTON CREEK

When you hike up Horton Creek, you enter an Eden tragically lost by an Arizona pioneer.

Fittingly, Horton Creek today is somewhat invisible — and that fact tends to keep away the crowds that congregate nearby. On weekends only a few find the delights of Horton, and on weekdays, a hiker might have the hidden haven all alone. And nowhere will the modern walker join the company of a more kindred spirit from a century ago.

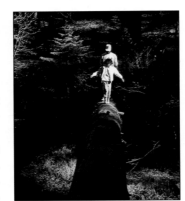

As a teenage boy, L.J. Horton with his sickly dad walked all the way from his home in Michigan to the promised land of California in 1863. By 1881, Horton, now married and 33 years of age, drifted into Arizona to establish a freighting business. As early as 1882 he located a ranch 20 miles to the east of Payson, on a tributary of Tonto Creek. In the copious manuscripts Horton later left to posterity, he described a lush refuge of grapevines and black walnuts, acres of wild iris and fields of native vegetables, a land flowing with milk and free honey — and unflagging neighbors.

By 1887 Horton "was milking 31 head of cows. I had not sold a steer or cow. I had kept all of my five years' increase. My freighting business paid all the expenses." He took an inventory and counted 211 head of beef cattle on his range. Then for a few months he had to journey south.

"I returned early in the spring...1888, heavily loaded with supplies. My trail wagon was loaded with fruit trees and shrubbery to beautify my place. All looked the same except that I saw no cattle. Neither did I see any signs of cattle around the salt lick.... I rode and searched the range for three months and failed to discover any cattle or any evidence. In July I gave my shrubbery to a neighbor.

"Once more in my life, like the blowing of a leaf, I am cast back with only the blind future to guide me. I never in all my wanderings had found a place that I learned to love so well."

Rustlers not only stole the cattle, but effectively they robbed Horton of the ability to make a living as a rancher. He was forced to abandon his claim and go back to freighting.

In frontiersman Horton's time, his creek flowed above ground to spill into Tonto. But early in this century the creek apparently cut its way through limestone to disappear into caverns which likely feed springs along the bigger Tonto Creek. So the first half-mile of hiking is past what appears to be an unpromising and barren dry wash.

But once to the water you'll encounter verdant creekside vegetation and picture postcard waterfalls. Exactly where Horton built his cabin and corrals is unknown, but several meadows with rock ruins are possibilities.

This trail (#285) offers options — an easy stroll up an old road above the creek, or a moderate hike along the creekside path, both ending at the springs where the creek originates. You also have the option of returning the way you came or hiking west (on the Highline Trail #31) to the junction of the Highline and the Hatchery Trail, 100 yards south of Tonto Fish Hatchery Road, FR 289. Whatever your choice, when you emerge from your journey to Horton's lost homestead, you'll fully appreciate a footnote he scribbled on his manuscript:

"In 1891 I got a letter from Mr. [Jesse] Ellison saying, 'Horton, I do not believe you have any cattle here. I herewith enclose eight dollars for one old cow.'

"That was all I got out of that five years' struggle." ■

Horton Creek
Trail Information

DIFFICULTY: Easy to moderate

TRAIL ACCESS: Drive east from Payson on State Route 260 just past Kohl's Ranch, turn left on FR 289 and go one mile to Upper Tonto Creek Campground. For the upper trailhead, continue on FR 289 about 2.5 miles to the end of the pavement at the Fish Hatchery Road. There the Hatchery Trail leads 100 yards to the south and connects with the Highline heading east to Horton Springs.

ELEVATION: 5,300 - 6,700 feet

DISTANCE: 4 miles one way to the springs. Distance from the springs to the hatchery is 3.4 miles.

HIKING TIME: 2-3 hours one way

SEASON: April-November

MARKED: Oak trail signs and well-used trail

WATER: Horton Creek and Horton Springs. Treat all water.

PARKING: Horton Trail — lot at Horton Picnic Ground across from Upper Tonto Campground. Hatchery Trail — Roadside at end of pavement (Fish Hatchery Road) at the Hatchery trailhead.

MANAGING AGENCY: Tonto National Forest.

(OPPOSITE PAGE) Nature provides a bridge at Horton Springs, just under the face of The Rim.
(BELOW) Moss-covered granite boulders, lush grass, beds of watercress and piney bowers beautify the grotto where Horton Creek rises at Horton Springs.
PHOTOGRAPHS BY NICK BEREZENKO

RIM CAMPING

It's hard to imagine anything in a lifetime that has changed so radically as how so many Americans camp. Two generations ago camping was primitive by comparison, with gear lashed to running boards and food preserved in cans. The highest tech marvel was a Coleman lantern.

Now in the nation a million campgrounds often as not boast electricity, water, and sewer hookups. Getting away from it all no longer is the game for many Americans. Clearly, they want to get closer to nature, but at the same time take the rough out of roughing it. Psychologists say the new breed of· camper is a child of the urban shift, uncomfortable and lonesome in too much space.

In a twist of irony, foresters consider the RV revolution to be the salvation of our woodlands. Their users do far less damage to the environment than those bygone bivouackers who chopped wood, fed warming and cooking fires, and buried garbage which animals promptly exhumed and scattered.

Yet the sheer numbers of people visiting Arizona's wooded refuges today are so multiplied — even considerate, contained, ethical camping is putting the land at risk.

Alarmed foresters and representatives set into motion the Arizona Recreation Initiative, now pumping a flood of funds into dozens of Forest Service projects and partnerships. The hope is that the new

Campgrounds

SITE NAME	APPROX. ELEV.	SEASONS OF USE	DAYS' LIMIT	FEE	NO. OF UNITS	SAFE WATER	REST-ROOMS	16 FT. RV LIMIT	WASTE DISP.	TABLE/ BENCH/ FIRE RING	BOATING	FISHING
ASPEN	7,500	MAY-SEPT.	14	X	136	X	X		X	X	X	X
BLACK CANYON RIM	7,600	MAY-SEPT.	14	X	21	X	X	X		X	X	X
BLUE RIDGE	7,300	MAY-SEPT.	14	X	10	X	X			X		
CANYON POINT	7,600	MAY-SEPT.	14	X	117	X	X		X	X		
CHEVELON CROSSING	6,300	MAR.-DEC.	14		7		X	X		X		X
CHRISTOPHER CREEK	5,600	MAY-SEPT.	7	X	43	X	X			X		X
CLINTS WELL	7,000	MAY-NOV.	14		7		X			X		
CROOK	7,600	MAY-SEPT	14	X	34	X	X		X		X	X
GENTRY	7,700	MAY-SEPT.	14		6		X	X		X		
KEHL SPRINGS	7,500	MAY-SEPT.	14		8		X			X		
KNOLL LAKE	7,500	MAY-SEPT.	14	X	33	X	X			X	X	X
MOGOLLON	7,600	MAY-SEPT.	14	X	32	X	X		X		X	X
PONDEROSA	5,600	MAY-SEPT.	7	X	61	X	X		X	X		
RIM	7,500	MAY-SEPT.	14	X	26	X	X				X	X
ROCK CROSSING	7,500	MAY-SEPT.	14	X	35	X	X			X	X	X
SINK HOLE	7,500	APRIL-OCT.	14	X	26	X	X			X	X	X
SPILLWAY	7,500	MAY-SEPT.	14	X	26	X	X		X	X	X	X
LOWER TONTO CREEK	5,400	ALL YEAR	7	X	17	X	X	X		X		X
UPPER TONTO CREEK	5,500	MAY-SEPT.	7	X	9	X	X	X		X		X
VALENTINE RIDGE	6,600	APRIL-NOV.	14		9		X	X		X		X

facilities will catch up with demand, and thereafter reasonable sums will keep the places and programs maintained and going.

But even if all this comes to pass, *you* are the key to success. Plan ahead. Honor signs. Stay on trails. Don't trench around tents. Kill fires. Follow sensible sanitation rules. Don't wash dishes or clean fish in lakes and streams. And regarding litter: Pack it in, and pack it out. Take from nature nothing but memories; leave nothing but footprints.

Then maybe the lyrical thought of John Muir will thrive into perpetuity: "I used to envy the father of our race, dwelling as he did in contact with the new-made fields and plants of Eden; but I do so no more, because I have discovered that I also live in creation's dawn. The morning stars still sing together, and the world, not yet half made, becomes more beautiful every day." ■

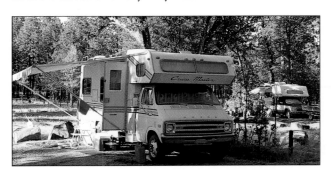

(ABOVE) A couple of America's 8.5 million recreation vehicles tarry a spell at the Forest Service's Aspen Campground near Woods Canyon Lake. It's estimated that nearly a million citizens a year now visit The Rim Country.
NICK BEREZENKO

Dispersed Camping Areas*

SITE NAME		APPROX. ELEV.	SEASONS OF USE	DAYS' LIMIT	NO. OF UNITS	REST-ROOMS	16 FT. RV LIMIT	BOATING	FISHING
AIRPLANE FLAT		6,600	APRIL-NOV.	14		X			X
BEAR CANYON LAKE		7,900	APRIL-OCT.	14		X		X	X
UPPER CANYON CREEK		6,600	APRIL-OCT.	14		X			X
CHEVELON LAKE		6,900	MAY-OCT.	14		X		X	X
COLCORD RIDGE		7,600	MAY-OCT.	14		X			
EAST VERDE COMPLEX	FLOWING SPG (FR 272)	4,600	APRIL-OCT.	14		X	X		X
	WATER WHEEL (FR 199)	4,900	APRIL-OCT.	14		X			X
	2ND X-ING (FR 199)	5,100	APRIL-OCT.	14		X	X		X
	3RD X-ING (FR 199)	5,150	APRIL-OCT.	14		X	X		X
	VERDE GLEN (FR 199)	5,300	APRIL-OCT.	14		X	X		X
FR 9350		7,600	MAY-SEPT.	14	42				
FR 195		7,600	MAY-SEPT.	14	20				
AL FULTON PT (FR 171)		7,600	APRIL-OCT.	14	50				
FR 300		7,700	APRIL-OCT.	14	29				
FR 169		7,700	APRIL-OCT.	14	5				

Almost all Rim Country campgrounds are first come, first served. However, you may make reservations at Aspen, Canyon Point, and Spillway campgrounds. Call toll-free 1-800-283-CAMP. It requires 10-days advance notice. You may pay the fee with credit card or check, but once you hang up the phone the transaction is final. When you arrive your spot will be waiting, according to the concessionaire.

* **Dispersed Camping Areas** have few facilities, no drinking water, and no fee. All camping must be self-contained. Go the extra mile — pack out more than you pack in.

Chapter Five

F ollowing your breath-stopping ascension to the top of The Rim, there opens a plateau of park-like woods, shallow lakes, rolling undulations, pancake flat cienegas, sinkholes, limestone ledges, and tentative little drainages.

Some spritzes of water leap off The Rim southward as intermittent falls, but most moisture seeks a gentler pull of gravity northward, eventually gathering to slice deep canyons bisecting the tablelands. Clear and Chevelon creeks, for example, dump topside runoff into the Little Colorado River. And both cloudburst and snowmelt ultimately may race northwestward another hundred miles before ramming west through the gut of Grand Canyon and on down the Colorado River.

On top. At Al Fulton Point the altimeter reads 7,600 feet, and you feel a sharper bite in the wind and sense a thinness of air. Forester Tim Grier knows a story about Al Fulton Point. He says Al and brother Harry dared to drive a herd of sheep through cattle range, and cowman Wilford Scarlett stampeded the flock toward a sinkhole. Poor Al fell in and died.

Says Tim: "The original headstone, now missing, read, 'Murdered in 1888,' *not* 'Shot in 1901' as the tombstone now reads."

East Atop The Rim

HIGH, WIDE, AND WILD

Tim recommends an easy, brief hike that rather typifies the relaxed lay of the land on the backside of The Rim. Signs lead away, along Crooks Trail, from the southeast corner of the Al Fulton Point parking lot. The trail progresses 2,200 feet to a small sign pointing the way another 600 feet to Al's grave. It's an easy walk, about a mile round trip. It's usually pleasant, April through November, and the parking lot overviews will leave you bug-eyed.

State Route 260 from Fulton to Heber narrows to two lanes, but the 22 miles sail across as pretty a highland as Arizona has to offer.

About three miles east of Fulton Point the Young Road,

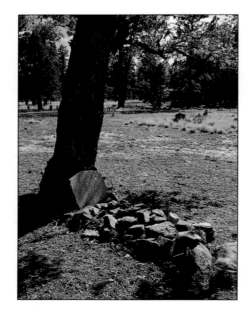

(OPPOSITE PAGE) Fir, pine, and oak form an almost unbroken mantle from Al Fulton Point to the distant Mazatzals. Now open at Fulton Point is a log-cabin Apache-Sitgreaves National Forest Visitor Center, where staffers share information for the entire Rim area. WESLEY HOLDEN
(RIGHT) Al Fulton's grave has a humble, inexpensive, handmade headstone, but it's near a million-dollar view. NICK BEREZENKO

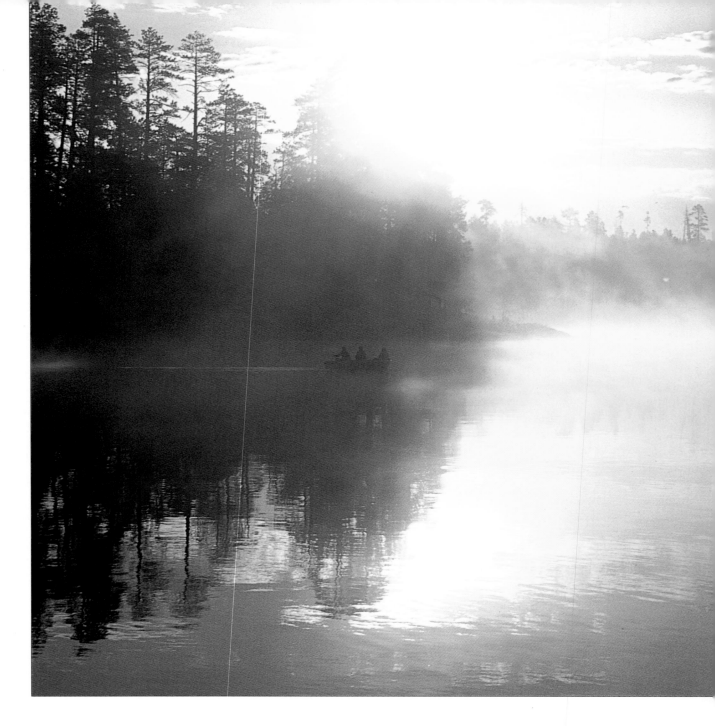

FR 512, goes south 3 miles to FR 33 which eases eastward to secluded Canyon Creek. Here the state operates another fish hatchery (open for tours), and this stream is limited to artificial fly and lure fishing only. Canyon was one of the first creeks set aside so that purist fly-casters should not have to compete side by side with more numerous bait anglers. A number of fly fishers go another step: using barbless hooks so that after the battle their catch may be easily released unharmed.

Back on State Route 260, as you proceed eastward you come to Forest Lakes, a sylvan community in and around the historic Long Tom spread. Forest Lakes holds a number of year-round residents as well as summer people. There's a restaurant, lodge, gas station, small grocery, and in winter cross-country skiing is in vogue. Forest Lakes Touring Center rents skis and grooms trails; when the snow vanishes, the action turns to canoeing and other sports.

Another cafe, named "The Rim," squats humbly at the side of the road in Heber. If you're in the neighborhood of a morning, try breakfast. Inside, the place is clean and the chow, delicious. That is, if you cotton to biscuits 'n' gravy, chicken-fried steak, and Denver omelets. Check out the bottle, tool, barbed wire, and pioneer portrait collections. Heber and satellite Overgaard have become service centers for hundreds of summer and retirement homes gracing the ridges and lining the shallow draws. While a thousand feet lower than the edge of The Rim, Heber still averages somewhat cooler temperatures than Payson.

Founded as a Mormon colony in 1876-77, Heber

Once a deep, rugged, remote chasm carved into the Colorado Plateau, Woods Canyon now contains an artificial lake that has offered fishing and boating for a generation of recreationists. The Woods Canyon Lake Recreation Area offers camping, RV services, boat rentals, groceries, beverages, and almost anything else the camper needs.
NICK BEREZENKO

maintains its village facade of industrious clutter and goes about its ranching, distribution, and retail businesses with the confident attitude of people living within their means. Some years Heber also throws one of Arizona's best summertime, small-town rodeos.

Elsewhere big-time cowboy tournaments are diluted by circus acts and glittering balladeers. When Heber competes, and at other towns on and under The Rim, rodeo casually survives in its original forms — riding, roping, and wrestling.

East of Overgaard about a mile begins a trip back to the violent history of the Old West. Just after crossing Pierce Wash, turn south off State Route 260 on Forest Road 144 for 2.8 miles. This is a good weather road. At FR 124 turn west and go a half mile. Turn south on FR 125 and go 2.6 miles to a large meadow which opens on your left.

Phoenix Park. It was named by James Stinson who owned the land and ran cattle on it in 1882. He had a home in Phoenix, and applied that name here. Stinson ran cattle in The Rim country as early as 1873 and owned a ranch to the north on Silver Creek which he sold to Mormon colonists who there founded the town of Snowflake.

Rustlers fighting over absentee-owner Stinson's herds led to one of the West's bloodiest range feuds, known as the Pleasant Valley War.

Before and after Stinson, Phoenix Park acquired a colorful history. General George Crook bivouacked his troops in this meadow during his Indian campaign. After Stinson, Daniel Boone Holcomb and his wife acquired the ranch at Phoenix Park (some maps still call the place Holcomb). The parents died, leaving their 14-year-old daughter, Sarah, who stayed on, ranching her entire life.

Today, elk bed down in the grassy meadow, a small spring seeps beneath giant cottonwoods on the west side, and the fireplace and foundation of Sarah's ranch house still stands. The ruins highlight a stroll around the large clearing.

Continue south two miles to FR 300, drive west 12 miles to Gentry Lookout, then a little less than two miles to the trailhead to where frontier justice failed (starts on the west side of Black Canyon Rim Campground).

Sometimes out West, they hanged the wrong men.

That happened atop The Rim more than a century ago. Three suspected horse thieves swung from the same tree...from the same limb.

The incident was an outgrowth of the Pleasant Valley War, adapted by Zane Grey for his novel *To the Last Man*. But no writer of fiction could rival the raw violence of this range war, also known as the Graham-Tewksbury Feud.

For 15 years, from the early 1880s to the late 1890s the war crackled around The Rim country like Mogollon sheet lightning. And before it wound down, certainly 30 men were dead. Possibly as many as 50. Thumbnails of the more sensational episodes:

Men were wounded as early as 1883, but the first to die was a shepherd in January 1887; apparently assassinated while camped north of Pleasant Valley. The Navajo herder was beheaded — perhaps as a warning to all sheepmen.

On a Sunday afternoon, September 4, 1887, in a one-street railroad stop named Holbrook north of The Rim, Sheriff Commodore Perry Owens (Commodore was his first name) stomped up onto the porch of a tiny frame house and demanded the surrender of one alleged rustler, Andy Cooper. By the time the gunfire ceased 30 seconds later Cooper and two other men were fatally shot and a fourth was crippled for life.

In the summer of 1888 the bushwhacking of Pleasant Valley settlers so intensified, the residents huddled together in a meadow commune, while two battle-ready companies of U.S. troops took up protective positions.

The last Graham to die was Tom. He was shot in the back (August 2, 1892) while driving a wagon load of grain to Tempe. His young widow concealed his sixshooter in her handbag, and when the courtroom was concentrating on testimony at a hearing for the alleged killer, she shoved the pistol into the side of the suspect and pulled the trigger. Misfire. The hammer caught on a fold of cloth.

The triple hanging atop The Rim was of still another kind of tragedy. James Stott, free-spirited, 25-year-old son of a prominent Massachusetts family, had established a horse ranch north of The Rim near Bear Springs. Generous financial support flowed from his parents. He had no need of other money. Had no cause to steal. Probably he crossed harm's way when northern Arizona sheepmen began to covet his water and range.

Sheepman and Deputy J.D. Houck and a small

SCOTT, SCOTT, AND WILSON GRAVESITE TRAIL INFORMATION

DIFFICULTY: Easy to moderate, rocky in places
TRAIL ACCESS: From mile marker 291.2 on State Route 260 turn south on Forest Road 300 2.8 miles to the oak trailhead sign on the north side of the road just past Black Canyon Rim Campground.

ELEVATION: 7,600 feet
DISTANCE: .7 mile one way
HIKING TIME: 45 minutes
SEASON: April-November
MARKED: Oak trail signs and blue diamond markers
WATER: None
PARKING: Roadside at trailhead
MANAGING AGENCY: Apache Sitgreaves National Forest

For more information on Stott, Scott, and Wilson and the Pleasant Valley War, read *A Little War of Our Own*, by Don Dedera, Prickly Pear Press, P.O. Box 42, Payson, AZ 85547.

posse surprised and took captive Jamie Stott and two cabin guests at Stott's Circle Dot Ranch headquarters at dawn on August 11, 1888 (not August 4, as on the modern headstones). The doomed men were put on horses and carried westward some miles when a large band of vigilantes called the "Committee of Fifty" threw down on the posse. The Committee took charge of the handcuffed and chained men, ran off the small posse, and continued westward on the Old Verde Road. (Old Verde Road, FR 166, is suitable for four-wheel-drive only. See map page 32-33.) They lynched the young men near present-day Black Canyon Rim Campground. All three bodies were found days later hanging from one stout bough of a ponderosa pine.

Every effort by Stott's parents to bring the vigilantes to justice was foiled by friends of the vigilantes. The perpetrators were never punished, except in their nightmares.

A short hike on a well-marked trail leads to the lovely glade where these men found their final rest.

From the gravesite trailhead, continue northwest on FR 300 to State Route 260. Turn left, west, 2 miles to Forest Lakes and turn north on FR 99.

Down and up, up and down. Think of two dozen baked baguettes, lying side by side...and together tilted slightly upward at one end. The long loaves of French bread make rounded ridges north and south, divided by ravines, the higher ends joined at The Rim. Now multiply your imagery by thousands. The mass of baguettes is the plateau, gently dropping down to the sagebrush flats of Coconino and Apache counties.

We begin our next driving adventure at Forest Lakes Estates. FR 99 heads north just a quarter-mile west of the Exxon station. Almost immediately half-hidden cabins give way to open greens commingling with clusters of conifers. Squirrels undulate out front, and a gilded flicker flashes over our hood. At 3.7 miles from the 260 turnoff, take a sharp left

(OPPOSITE PAGE) Most prominent remnant of Sara Holcomb's homestead at Phoenix Park is her chimney. WILLIAM E. BARCUS
(UPPER LEFT) The graves of Stott, Scott, and Wilson lie in a forest swale. WESLEY HOLDEN
(ABOVE LEFT) A black bear (cinnamon type) lumbers through ponderosa pine woodlands near West Clear Creek. WILLIAM E. BARCUS
(ABOVE RIGHT) A fat mule deer doe. WILLIAM E. BARCUS

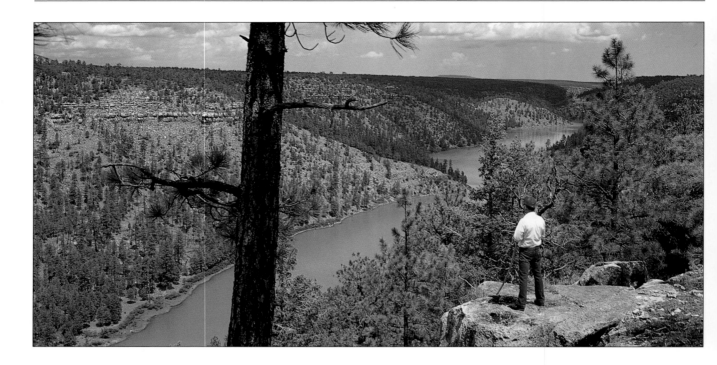

turn onto FR 170 and into specimen pines preserved as seedstock following recent logging. Arizona forests have never been clear-cut, and in this timber sale the trimmings (slash) are stacked for burning in a safer season. Soon a fresh generation of seedlings will replace the harvest. Never, ever, has the Forest Service planted so many trees as in recent years.

Then there! To the left! Twelve elk cows with their maturing young lope like a freight train through the glen. My companion, an Eastern-raised woman, may have a heart attack.

"These are part of a 10,000 herd," I say, as the elk keep pace with our Blazer. "They're on the increase. It's one of America's ecological tragedy/victory stories. During frontier times the original Merriam elk gave way to human occupation of The Rim Country. They disappeared. Hunting? Loss of range to cow grazing? Introduced disease? Those elk over there are the descendants of several transplants of Rocky Mountain elk from Yellowstone between 1913 and 1928."

There is not much difference in appearance of the two elk types. We groan when our road bends away from the cruising herd. They, in their flanking maneuver, had given not one inch of ground.

It is a little more than nine miles from the highway to FR 90. We decide to take a side trip. From here on it's a four-wheel-drive and high-center road. Since we have the appropriate vehicle, we follow George Pemberton's advice and slowly grind four

miles northwest to Weimer Point (at .5 mile take the right fork, at 2.5 miles the left). We pass through the eastern portion of the 4,000 acre Slim Fire. It is interesting to see how quickly the forest is recovering since the campfire-caused blaze swept through the area July 4, 1987. We park in a convenient turnaround area and walk the last .3 mile, as the four-wheel-drive road becomes more trail-like. Abruptly, Chevelon Canyon Lake appears: a glistening blue surprise, where eagles soar on thermals, and with binoculars you can look for big fish lolling in the shallows. If your car can't take a rough road, consider parking it and walk in and out. It takes a good half day (take water) and makes a great picnic hike.

Proceeding north on FR 170 toward Chevelon Crossing, we drive slowly, watching for deer, turkey, or javelina to cross the gravel road. The land continues to lose altitude and pines give way to cedar breaks. Just before linking up with FR 504 and turning west, an extensive example of juniper eradication dominates the landscape. It is done to give range grass a better chance.

(ABOVE) This spectacular overlook awaits adventurers who hike or four-wheel drive to Weimer Point above Chevelon Canyon Lake. The lake, however, is inaccessible from this point.
(OPPOSITE PAGE) Waders and anglers test the placid Chevelon Creek at historic Chevelon Crossing.
PHOTOGRAPHY BY
NICK BEREZENKO

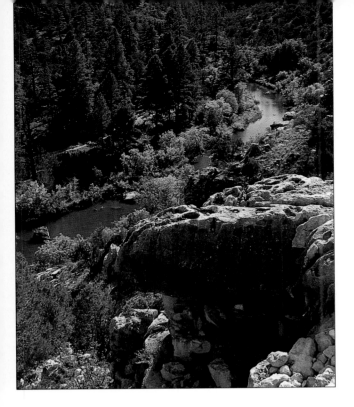

Because of steep hairpin turns, this road is limited to vehicles no more than 35 feet in length. The narrow, corduroy road dictates slow speed down to the one-lane bridge over the placid stream, where three trucks are parked. They are the only vehicles we have seen all morning. From the highway at Forest Lakes it is 24 miles to the wrinkled canyon walls at Chevelon Crossing (not including the side trip to Weimer Point).

As we wind our way up the west side of the canyon, we pass a small campground with ramadas and table-bench units (campsite limit 35 feet). Perfect for the camper/fisherman. Just past the crest of the hill, on the left, a track leads off to the remains of the CCC camp that once housed the young men who built this road, bridge, and campground.

At 26 miles is FR 169, and we turn sharply left. Now heading southwest, the road begins to climb and the scenery is reversed, from scrubby cedars and piñons we nuzzle back into the big pines. Piñon jays. Indian paintbrush. More deer. And linkup with the General Crook Trail FR 300 at aptly named Alder Lake for a total of 47 miles. What a day.

But in the opinion of others, there are even better days, days of autumn color. One morn all is green; next day, among the evergreens, a riot of leathery browns, ruby, saffron, crimson, burgundy. Scrub oaks tint entire slopes. Aspens splurge their gold dollars. Sumacs blaze. Elders wax flaxen. It was Albert Camus who said: "Autumn is a second spring when every leaf is a flower."

There exists a human scale and perspective in autumn that is somehow diminished in the gaudy promise of spring and the gross plenitude of summer. Here, between first frost and first snowfall, likely live the greatest percentage of people who don't give a damn if the dollar buys fewer yen, if neckties narrow or widen, and civilization elsewhere declines. It is time to core an apple and think a worthwhile thought. ∎

WHEN YOU GO...

Heber Ranger Station
P.O. Box 968, Overgaard, AZ
85933, (602) 535-4481
Chevelon Ranger Station
H-C 62, Box 600 Highway 99 South
Winslow, AZ 86047, (602) 289-2471
Pleasant Valley Ranger Station
P.O. Box 450
Young Az. 85554
Heber Chamber of Commerce
P.O. Box 550
Heber, AZ 85928
Food and services can be found at
Forest Lakes and Heber Overgaard.

NICK BEREZENKO

R I M L A K E S

When Europeans first arrived, Arizona had but one permanent lake — a basin of snowmelt inside a collapsed volcano near Flagstaff. Today there are some 200 sizeable artificial reservoirs within the state. They range from vast inland seas to municipal water impoundments; none is more handsome than The Rim's string of ponds, including:

Bear Canyon Lake — Not much used, Bear Canyon is many an avid angler's favorite. The well-built but steep trail discourages the faint of heart and weak of leg. Fishing is limited to flies and artificial lures. Sixty acres of turquoise water hold rainbows and brookies, some cutthroat and arctic grayling. Strict fishing regulations apply. The pretty, dispersed camping area is ringed by aspens. Access is via State Route 260 to the Woods Canyon Lake turnoff, then west on FR 300 for 15 miles to FR 89 — north three miles to the lake site-entrance, then switchback a mile to the head of the lake.

Black Canyon Lake — A continuation of unpaved FR 300 departs Highway 260 at milepost 291.2, which is about two miles east of Forest Lakes Estates. The road can be slick and muddy after rains.

Bank casting after rainbows and browns is customary. There's a paved ramp and the Black Canyon Rim Campground, 21-units, is about two miles from the lake.

Blue Ridge Reservoir — A commercial purpose justified a dam at the confluence of East Clear Creek and General Springs Canyon. A 160-foot high concrete barrel-arch structure, first of its kind in the United States, forms a narrow lake. When full, Blue Ridge Reservoir covers over 200 acres. The deal between Phelps Dodge and the Salt River Project allowed the mining firm to take project water in eastern Arizona and pay it back with water from north of The Rim. Two bonuses: The pay-back water runs down the East Verde, ensuring a strong, steady flow; and the reservoir affords splendid recreation. Mostly rainbows but a few big brownies populate the fishery. Nearby campgrounds include 10-unit Blue Ridge, 7-unit Clints Well, and 35-unit Rock Crossing. (See map pages 32-33) Access: State Route 87, 4.5 miles north of Clint's Well; the good but unpaved FR 751 goes about six miles east to the reservoir.

Chevelon Lake — This is one of the largest and

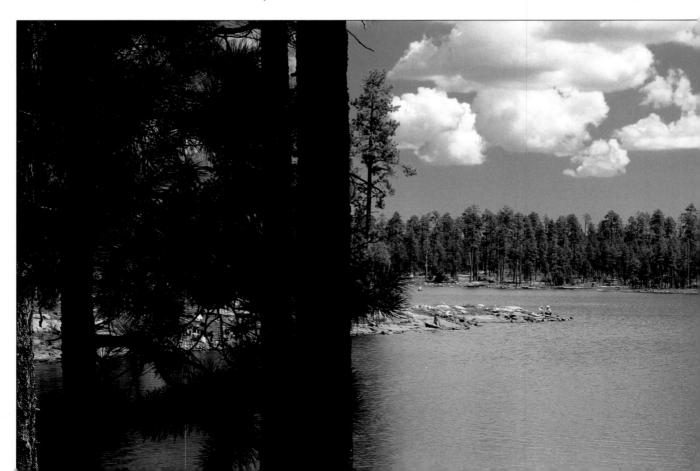

most difficult to get to of all The Rim lakes. Its nearly 200 acres wind through incredibly beautiful steep canyon walls for nearly three miles. When dam construction was started in the early 1960s, the first order of business was a road to the site. Since the lake was completed, the road has slowly deteriorated and is now a trail only. Even FR 169B, which takes visitors and fisherman past Chevelon Lake Campground on the top of the canyon, is difficult — almost impossible in stormy conditions. Access: From State Route 260, take Woods Canyon Lake turnoff and FR 300 eight miles westerly to FR 169. Turn right, northeasterly, 11.5 miles to FR 169B, the Chevelon Lake turnoff, then 1.5 miles to the parking area. From there it's a steep one mile walk on a well-marked trail to the lake.

Knoll Lake — A high lake at 7,900 feet, Knoll extends two arms to cover 75 acres of East Leonard Canyon. Its name comes from a little, knoll-like island, ideal for picnicking. As in most Rim Country lakes, stocked rainbows far outnumber big browns. Electric trolling motors only, allowed. Knoll Lake Campground, 33 units, usually is uncrowded Monday through Thursday, but jampacked on summer weekends. The access (FR 295E) tees off of FR 300 24 miles west of Highway 260. The road to the lake is 4.5 miles long and rough.

Willow Springs Lake — The epitome of ease in access, a paved road at milepost 283 on Highway 260 leads 1.4 miles to the 80-acre lake. A paved ramp facilitates launches of boats with motors of not more than eight horsepower. The quarry: rainbows and brown trout (some big ones). Sink Hole campground, 26-units, is less than a mile away.

Woods Canyon Lake — The beginning of The Rim's bounteous artificial recreation lakes, 52-acre Woods Canyon was dammed in 1956 and filled that winter. It has become one of Arizona's most popular and best developed water recreation areas: store, boat rental, picnic area, five large-to-medium campgrounds, an encircling hike and a nature trail. Catchable trout are stocked directly from the hatchery. Access: State Route 260 east of Payson to the Woods Canyon Lake turnoff at the top of The Rim. From there it's five paved miles to the lake. ■

On a turquoise pond in an emerald forest under a cobalt sky filled with opal clouds, a raft drifts across Willow Springs Lake.
BOB CLEMENZ

Chapter Six

One of the very first travelers across The Rim was a remarkable woman. In late summer 1872, Martha Summerhayes joined her soldier husband and rode in a military wagon (called an ambulance) from Fort Mohave on the Colorado River to the territorial capital of Prescott, then continued 150 miles farther eastward across the Rim Country to Fort Apache. At the time, she was six months pregnant.

Many years later, safe in her New England home, she gathered up her notes and recollections and wrote her immortal classic, *Vanished Arizona*.

The initial 40-mile pull from Prescott to Fort Verde, on the Verde River, was a walk in the park, but from there the "road" was all but impassable. It heaved and curved to Thirteen Mile Rock where a ramp only slightly wider than the wagon track literally had been carved into the face of that solid monolith. The grade was so steep that soldiers had to throw their shoulders into the wheels to assist the mules that already were double- and triple-teamed.

She penned in 1908: "The traveling was very difficult and rough, and both men and animals were worn out by night. But we were now in the mountains, the air was

West Atop The Rim
WHERE THE FIRST WHEELS TURNED

cool and pleasant, and the nights so cold that we were glad to have a small stove in our tents to dress by in the mornings. The scenery was wild and grand; in fact, beyond all that I had ever dreamed of; more than that, it seemed so untrod, so fresh, somehow, and I do not suppose that even now, in the day of railroads and tourists, many people have had the view of the Tonto Basin which we had one day from the top of the Mogollon range." The cavalcade fed itself from the

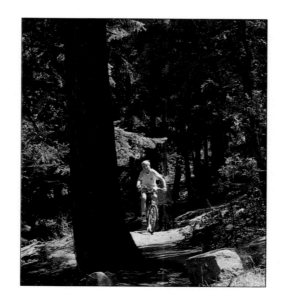

(OPPOSITE PAGE) Quaking aspens don their autumn dress. Beavers used to dam the waters of Bear Canyon atop The Rim. Today a bigger dam, built by humans, transforms the canyon into a fly fisherman's paradise.
(RIGHT) Mountain bicycling offers a different way to negotiate the Woods Canyon Lake Trail.
PHOTOGRAPHY BY NICK BEREZENKO

land: antelope, turkey, deer. Martha Summerhayes and her trooper Jack reached Fort Apache after two months of continuous travel.

Today this journey over General Crook's Road conceivably could be accomplished in a few hours by passenger car — more remarkable in that contemporary highways and byways closely follow the original. And that the appearance of the land and its life are so similar to those of 120 years ago. Thanks for this belongs in large measure to the setting aside as undeveloped public lands the Coconino National Forest, encompassing the Mogollon Plateau on the west and Apache and Sitgreaves national forests on the east.

In the Rim Country, FR 300, improved in 1928, frequently intersects the old military road. In common with the old, the newer, better graded but still unpaved route dips and weaves across the densely

wooded, irregular Mogollon, here leaving The Rim to visit fir-and-aspen glades, there skirting the very edge of the plateau. Out there was where Captain George M. Wheeler marveled:

"Mountain, forest, valley, and streams are blended in one harmonious whole...few worldwide travelers in a lifetime could be treated to a more perfect landscape, a true virgin solitude, undefiled by the presence of man."

The military road was the strategic penetration of the most remote realm of the fierce Apaches, who in their zenith terrorized a region larger than Germany and France combined. Over this crucial supply line George C. Crook not only supported distant outposts, but dropped off fighting units to raid Apache camps throughout Tonto Basin. It required a decade of intense campaigning, but in the end no haven of warrior Apaches was secure from the troops and Indian scouts faithfully serving General George Crook. In respect, the Apaches named Crook, Gray Wolf.

The green, young enlisted men who scratched the road across The Rim measured miles by counting the revolutions of a wagon wheel. Every time a white-painted spoke came around, a soldier

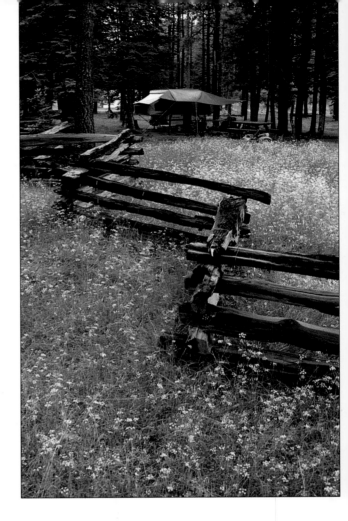

dropped a pebble into a bucket. At each mile they chiseled the number into a boulder or carved it into a tree. The vast wildness of the Mogollon Rim and the threat of Indian attack worried these young men who were mostly from the East or had recently immigrated from Europe. To ensure they didn't lose their way these raw recruits blazed a remarkable number of trees along the trail at intervals so close a blaze was never out of sight. The dot-dash, like an inverted exclamation point on the fronts and backs of trees on both sides of the road, showed the way.

Numerous blazed trees, ancient even then, still line the road, which in sections faintly shows as ruts across slickrock and shallow cuts along slopes. In 1975, the Boy Scouts of Northern Arizona adopt-

(LEFT) On his favorite mule, Maude, General George C. Crook campaigned with his Apache Indian scouts. COURTESY ARIZONA HISTORICAL SOCIETY
(ABOVE) Split rail fence, Kehl Springs Campground. Nick Berezenko
(OPPOSITE PAGE) The word "vertical" assumes full meaning on the edge of The Rim at Hi View Point. Nick Berezenko
(FOLLOWING PANEL) South from The Rim seven distinct ridgelines can be counted. DICK DIETRCH

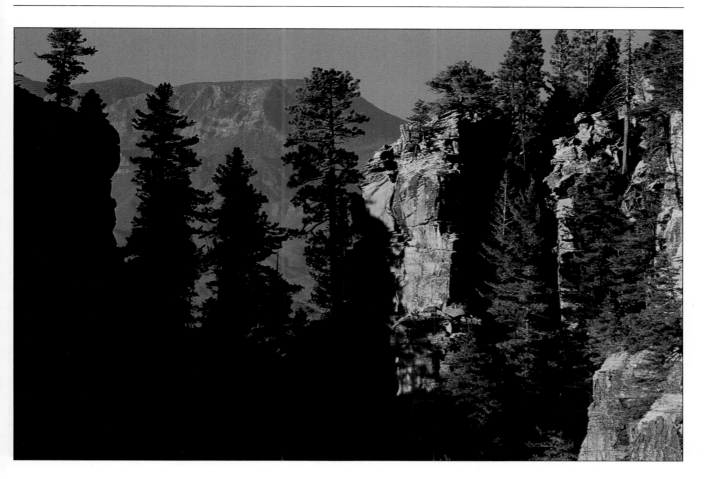

ed Crook's Trail as their Bicentennial project. Where many markings were missing, lads of many troops erected posts bearing chevrons. They also placed chevrons on surviving blazed trees, so that every one of the 135 miles that Crook's road traverses public land, is marked for you.

Forest Road 300 is the east-west connector from which scores of other forest roads and foot trails head north or south. Generally north-running routes head gently downhill through a swatch of forest 20 to 30 miles wide. Southerly foot trails drop steeply off The Rim. Forest Road 300 wants to be driven leisurely, easy on the springs, tires, and passengers. Some of the roads that T northward are better negotiated in four-wheel drive or high-clearance truck. And where the runoff gathers and cuts deep canyons in its rush to the Colorado River, some ways are simply not passable. Not even jackass-able. It pays to inquire locally, particularly in wet seasons.

With that caveat, here are some of the things and places you can do and visit on the western portion of the Mogollon Rim:

Blue Ridge Reservoir, Knoll Lake, and Bear

Canyon Lake — (For complete information, see "Rim Lakes Guide," page 52-53.)

Barbershop Canyon — As one admirer has written, "This canyon contains more wildlife than many zoos." Several roads and hiking trails descend the ledges of this scenic canyon, and other paths lead to Dick Hart and Dane ridges. Because of the elemental land forms and changeable road conditions, it's best to make inquiry at the Blue Ridge Ranger Station near the intersection of State Route 87 and FR 95, (602) 477-2255. The rewards are worth the effort, but clambering about this bit of backwoods requires smart planning and reasonably good health.

Baker Butte Fire Tower — Exactly 10.4 miles north of Strawberry, State Route 87 crosses the General Crook Trail (FR 300). Then 1.4 miles east, FR 300 leads to a right turnoff through a gate. Climb rocky switchbacks to the top of the butte. At 8,034 feet this is the highest point on The Rim. In low gear you will urge your vehicle along forest floors lush with fern, wild strawberry, columbine, and cliff rose. Oaks and conifers crowd the narrow canyons and march along the ridges to the clearing around

the tower. There's been a lookout on Baker Butte since the teen years of this century, when men with binoculars perched on the limb of a pine and shouted alarms over a rudimentary telephone. If the guard is not busy, you may go up. On a clear day, Camelback Mountain marks Phoenix, 85 airline miles southwest. Southeasterly, on crystal clear days, you can see the top of the Santa Catalina Mountains at Tucson. Look north and see the Hopi mesas. In all, the view totals 250 miles! Tiny but beautiful 8-unit Kehl Springs Campground is nearby.

The Cabin Loop System — Connecting three early day Forest Service structures with pathways and telephone, the system once fed fire and other information into the Long Valley Ranger Station. The loop and surviving structures today lie within the Blue Ridge Ranger District. At elevations around 7,500 feet, the Cabin Loop circulates through some

cherishes warming memories: The place was named for General George Crook. Cook's dad worked for the Forest Service. And, "that log house was about 25 years old when we lived there. It was a cozy home, especially in the evening when we read or played cards by the light of a Coleman lantern, or listened to Fibber McGee on the battery-powered radio. The outhouse was over the hill. We carried water in galvanized pails from the spring, 50 yards from the cabin." In 1989 the Forest Service restored the structure. Access: east of State Route 87, 12 miles on FR 300. The cabin is only a half mile north of FR 300 from the monument commemorating the Battle of Big Dry Wash.

Buck Springs Fire Guard Station — Two cabins, one dating to 1923, are still used during high risk months by firefighters. Only the site remains of the very first Buck Springs cabin built in the early

of the plateau's most spectacular scenery: ever-flowing springs, diverse geological features, and rich foliation. The trails that connect these cabins cross miles of forest terrain and are not for the inexperienced hiker. For more information on these trails contact the above ranger district, or get a copy of "The Mogollon Rim Hiking Map" available for $3.95 from *Arizona Highways*, 2039 West Lewis Avenue, Phoenix, AZ 85009.

You can drive to each of the cabins which include:

General Springs Cabin — James E. Cook, who in the 1940s lived in this cabin for five summers,

1900s. Access to the station from FR 300 is 4.2 miles via FR 137 and right .7 of a mile on FR 137D.

Pinchot Cabin — Gifford Pinchot (1865-1946) was a trailblazing forester and conservationist who led the U.S. Forest Service from 1898 to 1910 and inspired many of its early conservation policies. He visited the site and remarked upon its beauty. Foresters named the place for their nature-defending leader. Several now-vanished cabins preceded this one, built in the 1930s by a fire guard. Access: State Route 87 to Blue Ridge Ranger Headquarters, south on FR 95 11 miles, then left on FR 139A, .2 mile. Pinchot Cabin will be on your left.

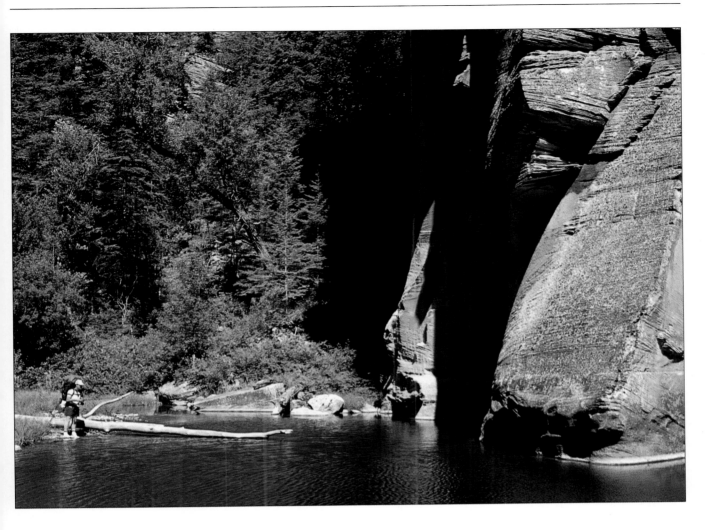

(OPPOSITE PAGE, LEFT) Along the Cabin Loop Trail hikers encounter this old line shack of a ranching operation. WILLIAM E. BARCUS
(OPPOSITE PAGE, RIGHT) Long and very deep, Blue Ridge Reservoir was created to effect a water trade from one Rim Country drainage to another. WILLARD CLAY
(ABOVE) Grotesque rock formations await hikers to West Clear Creek Wilderness. NICK BEREZENKO

West Clear Creek Wilderness — Road access to this wilderness area is difficult, and the steep hiking trail even more so. Nevertheless, experienced outdoorspeople will find West Clear Creek to be pristine, with fern-covered grottoes, deep crystalline pools, and springs protected from the rest of the world by 700 foot high canyon walls. But go fully prepared, and be sure someone on the outside knows where you're going. An accident here would leave you *very* alone. Access: State Route 87 to Clints Well, north on FH 3 about seven miles to the West Clear Creek sign. Turn west on FR 81 another seven miles (continuing straight ahead onto FR 81E when

the road splits) until it ends. Four wheel drive from here. Turn left on FR 140, .5 mile then right on FR 140E two miles to road's end. The trailhead is marked with a sign and rock cairn. It is recommended you contact Beaver Creek Ranger Station before entering the wilderness area.

Battle of Big Dry Wash — It was the last pitched battle between substantial numbers of Apaches and U.S. Troops.

In late spring, 1882, firebrand Nan-tia-tish and his band bolted the San Carlos Apache reservation and raided below The Rim in Pleasant Valley. They stole horses, murdered prospectors, wounded ranchers, and burned buildings. A few days later, with as many as 250 adult warriors, Nan-tia-tish beset the Meadows Ranch on the East Verde. They killed the father and wounded two sons, one fatally.

But the Indians' days were numbered. Forces converged from several directions. Feeling invincible, the renegades dawdled northward. By July 16 soldiers from five Arizona army posts pressed the renegades up onto the Tonto Rim. Suspecting a trap near General Springs, the soldiers set one of their own. With Major Adna R. Chaffee as battle commander, the soldiers and their Indian scouts on July 17 baited the Indians with a column of cavalry on white horses. Then while the Indians were distracted, other units outflanked them down Battleground Ridge.

In the ensuing close-quarter combat, Apache fatalities numbered about 22. On the army side, one Apache scout was killed and several soldiers wounded. Had not a severe, high-country thunder and hail storm obscured the battlefield for 20 minutes, Indian losses surely would have been greater.

The battle area is honored by a second monument. But historians now are convinced the actual battle occurred on the ridge across the canyon from the marker. For many years the ground all about was littered by spent ammunition, lost and broken equipment, and ration containers: thus the name, Crackerbox Canyon. ■

Battle of Big Dry Wash Battle Area Trail Information

DIFFICULTY: Easy
TRAIL ACCESS: Take FR 300 about 11.8 miles east from State Route 87, then follow the signs north on FR 123 about seven miles, taking the left fork where indicated. Monument is .25 mile beyond road's end. Actual battle area is another .5 mile.
ELEVATION: 7,000 - 6,600 feet
DISTANCE: .75 mile one way
HIKING TIME: 45 minutes round trip
SEASON: May-October
MARKED: Lack of a sign makes it a little difficult to find, but the trail is easy to follow. There are two bronze plaques at the monument.
WATER: None
PARKING: Roadside at end of road
MANAGING AGENCY: Coconino National Forest

WHEN YOU GO...

Between Strawberry and the northern boundary of Coconino National Forest, facilities are few along State Route 87. About midway is the picturesque little crossroads of Clints Well. Forest Highway 3 presents a handsome high-country drive northwestward past big lakes to Flagstaff. Clints Well facilities have food and fuel.

Coconino National Forest
2323 East Greenlaw Lane
Flagstaff, AZ 86004
(602) 556-7400
Blue Ridge Ranger District, H-C 31
P.O Box 300
Happy Jack, AZ 86024
(602) 477-2255 or 556-7375
Long Valley Ranger District, H-C 31
P.O Box 68
Happy Jack, AZ 86024
(602) 354-2216
Arizona Game & Fish Department
2222 West Greenway
Phoenix, AZ

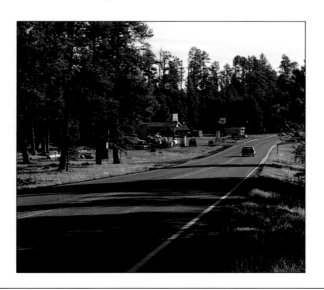

(LEFT) Clints Well, where Forest Highway 3 joins State Route 87, offers Rim Country adventurers an outpost in the vast expanses of Coconino National Forest.
(OPPOSITE PAGE) Mouth of the Mineral Belt Tunnel.
PHOTOGRAPHS BY NICK BEREZENKO

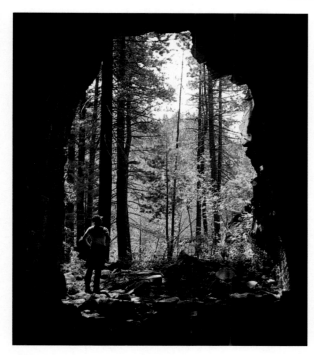

One of Arizona's oddest early-day episodes involved big dreams, daring gambles, high hopes, numbing toil, and ultimate defeat.

The scheme to pierce the Mogollon Rim with a railroad tunnel was the brainchild of Chicago attorney and entrepreneur James W. Eddy. In its most grandiose extension, the Arizona Mineral Belt Railroad would traverse the entirety of the territory, south to north, from the Mexican border near Nogales to the Utah border near Lees Ferry. By its intersection with the Southern Pacific in the south and the Atlantic & Pacific in the north, the Mineral Belt would transform Tucson and Flagstaff into major railroad hubs.

Those were the easy parts.

The tough nut to crack: The Rim.

But capital was raised, and engineers advanced a plan. A bore of 3,100 feet, 16 feet wide at the bottom and 20 feet high, would take advantage of a natural notch in The Rim north of Payson. The anticipated destination through the sandstone was General Springs Canyon atop The Rim.

Work began by a crew of 40 in August 1883.

In something more than a month the drillers made 70 feet of hole. Then Eddy ran out of money and work stopped.

Over the next decade an agony of refinancing, track laying, back stabbing, and suing plagued the Mineral Belt. In time the grand concept was abandoned, leaving not much but some miles of roadbed on fairly level ground near Flagstaff, and The Tunnel to Nowhere on The Rim. ∎

Tunnel to Nowhere Trail Information

DIFFICULTY: Difficult, steep with loose footing in places

TRAIL ACCESS: Take Forest Road 300, 12 miles east from its junction with State Route 87 to the Battle of Big Dry Wash monument. Start at the small trailhead sign on the south side of FR 300. Descend 100 feet to the second pole, then turn left to the east side of the canyon. Continue approximately .5 mile to the next small sign where the trail fishhooks to the left and starts back up The Rim to the tunnel. This last .25 mile of trail is steep, very rocky, and somewhat difficult to follow.

ELEVATION: 7,200 feet

DISTANCE: 1.5 miles roundtrip

HIKING TIME: 2-3 hours

SIGNAGE: Small trail signs

WATER: None

PARKING: Roadside at Battle of Big Dry Wash monument

SEASONS: April-November

MANAGING AGENCY: Coconino and Tonto national forests

For a more complete story, see "A Vision of Grandeur: The Arizona Mineral Belt Railroad," by Robert A. Trennert, *Arizona and the West,* quarterly published by the University of Arizona Press, Winter, 1970.

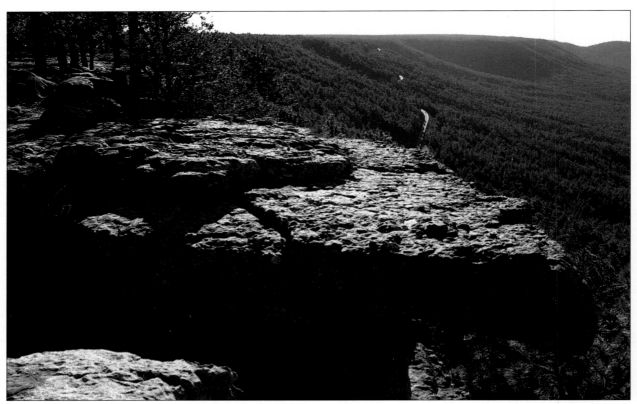

FRANK ZULLO

Arizona's uplands are crisscrossed by a modern motoring spectrum from four-lane highways to four-wheel drive trails. Here are some tips:

Stay tuned to weather news — At higher altitude, Arizona's climate is wetter, cooler, and stormier. Official advisories include warnings of winds whose gusts can give high profile vehicles trouble. Unpaved roads can become slick and gummy following rain showers and thaws.

Slow down — Inquire locally about road conditions.

Take chains or snow tires—They are often required by the Highway Patrol October through April when slush or ice slicken blacktop. Back roads can become partly frozen quagmires.

Check automobile fluids — Temperatures may swing 40 degrees from day to night. Liquid cooled engines need antifreeze protection during colder seasons. So does your windshield washing water.

Top off your gas tank — Uphill can double fuel consumption. In places, it's a far piece between service stations.

Learn the log truck duck — It's a handy maneuver for defensive driving off paved road. On sighting an approaching rig, slow down, skirt to the right side, and pray that a flying stone will not ding your windshield or headlamps.

Beware of creek crossings — even dry ones. Flash flooding can result from faraway storms.

Be alert — Wildlife and range cattle frequent roadways, often at night.

Share your plans — with somebody who cares. If you don't show up, that should start a search. ■

(BACK COVER) Feisty
rainbows and a few large
brown trout attract anglers
to Blue Ridge Reservoir.
NICK BEREZENKO